"Robin shows us the way to being a clear channel for the Divine and how it opens doors to a life of meaning, peace and purpose. Step by step in Part 1 of the book, you will be taken down the road of enlightenment through the tools of life coaching. You are in good hands with Robin"

Mika Heilmann,
Coach, Teacher and Writer
Denmark

"This book has touched me very deeply since amazingly enough after reading I was able to heal a wound which I didn't even know had been anchored in my emotional body. Written in a simple and fluid style, this book is bound to attract and inspire an incredible number of readers, way beyond these shores. And, for me, it is a true honor to partake in its publication, therefore participating in the spiritual evolution of the human race. This is a wonderful time to be alive and to witness humanity slowly coming back to the oneness of its true nature. Indeed, we are one."

Danielle Bonnefil-Wahab
Teacher, Tri-Lingual Translator
Haiti/USA

"In Peru, Robin and I met in an usual fashion with her awareness beyond this world as she touched me deeply with her wisdom. We are both from African soil and share a path where there are no tracks. Robin, you truly live what you teach."

Adele Green
Coach, Kinesiologist and Writer
South Africa

"To live in the NOW is in every moment to be aware and one with all elements, to honor them and their being. We are all one, inside and outside. To live in the NOW it is necessary to be in unity with our highest. As described in this book, this new way of being is a way of healing our past and creating a new future where all things are done in love and with self-love."

Uta Bolduan
Teacher, Writer
Germany

Awakening of a
Chocolate Mystic

Robin L. Johnson

BALBOA
PRESS

A DIVISION OF HAY HOUSE

Balboa Press books may be ordered through booksellers or by contacting:

Balboa Press
A Division of Hay House
1663 Liberty Drive
Bloomington, IN 47403
www.balboapress.com
1-(877) 407-4847

Because of the dynamic nature of the Internet, any web addresses or
links contained in this book may have changed since publication and
may no longer be valid. The views expressed in this work are solely those
of the author and do not necessarily reflect the views of the publisher,
and the publisher hereby disclaims any responsibility for them.

The author of this book does not dispense medical advice or prescribe the use
of any technique as a form of treatment for physical, emotional, or medical
problems without the advice of a physician, either directly or indirectly. The
intent of the author is only to offer information of a general nature to help
you in your quest for emotional and spiritual well-being. In the event you use
any of the information in this book for yourself, which is your constitutional
right, the author and the publisher assume no responsibility for your actions.

Cover: Photo of the Gulf of Finland taken by author Robin L. Johnson

ISBN: 978-1-4525-3303-2 (sc)
ISBN: 978-1-4525-3304-9 (e)
Library of Congress Control Number: 2011923097

Printed in the United States of America
Balboa Press rev. date: 4/5/2011

To my Mother,
"Thanks for being a bridge over troubled waters"

"For years people have spoken of the "Age of Aquarius" as being a time of global oneness, as we experience "love and light". Could that time be now? Could those people be us?"

Robin L. Johnson

Contents

Foreword

"Awakening of a Chocolate Mystic" made me realize why chocolate is so essential to my daily diet. Perhaps the divine pleasure I get from its scrumptious taste reminds me, as this profound book has, of why we need both bitter and sweet ingredients to create a delicious life.

In Part I, Robin has given us the tools and a clear roadmap on how to "clean out the vessel" so that you can give God "room to operate" within you so that life will flow more freely. This way you are aligning with the spirit of all that is, all that was and all that ever will be. Once you are aligned with this spirit you are in what many call "the flow." You will soon find yourself with people and in places you never dreamed you could be. It's the place of synchronicities and "aha" moments and soon you will feel you cannot live any other way.

Through sharing her own life experiences Robin clearly spells out what we need to do to awaken to a life as a Chocolate Mystic beginning with grounding oneself in spiritual concepts (by reading spiritual and personal growth books, attending sessions with Modern Masters etc.) so you can gain a new perspective (worldview) and "build your faith in your own transformation as well as creating the foundation for forgiveness for the faults and frailties in others."

She advises us to seek a place of stillness so you can hear the spirit of God and follow guidance. This way we will move from a thought system controlled by the "ego" to one that is guided by spirit. She encourages us to harmonize our feeling nature by "accepting our authentic emotionality". To get real with our emotions and not feel that if we express emotions like anger or resentment we don't become enlightened. In fact, Robin assures us that by expressing them we will be on the path to building a truly authentic life. And what better way to build this life than to master our appetites for pleasures and addictions.

I remember reading the first section of this book titled "Bitter" and feeling grateful to Robin for having the courage to publically disclose her story…the rape as a young child, an adulterous affair, an abortion and illegal drug use. She put it all out there not wishing for "the ego to continue to have a hiding place." This liberation gave the mystical side space to appear. We spend so much energy trying to hide who we really are and this blocked energy prevents the circulation of that effortless flow that comes from living a truly authentic life.

Modern Mystics are ordinary people who take on the spiritual assignment to clear their channels, master their appetites for life and open themselves up to direct guidance from the Spirit of God, the Divine. When the Modern Mystic gets "the call" there's no stopping the sequence of events that will set in motion your next spiritual experience. So I knew I was in for quite a journey especially with a tour leader like Gregg Braden that encouraged us to listen to our spirit as we embarked on this very special journey to Peru.

We arrived in Peru the land of the Incas, Andes, sacred site of Machu Picchu and Lake Titicaca…and also the land that has drawn numerous "Mystic Travelers" who felt pulled to take a journey to this mysterious place. Members of our group just "knew" there was some reason why they all needed to go to Peru and arranged their lives to get there.

One day a very friendly woman, Robin Johnson came up to me and said she would love for us to have the opportunity to chat one day because she also had a great deal of experience dealing with international organizations, like I had with the United Nations. I said "sure, I would love to" but then with the busyness of our tour, days turned into nights without us having the chance to speak. Something inside me kept saying "you need to speak to Robin" and it didn't take long for me to realize that there was more to this. When spirit speaks to you, you know it. There's a depth of being that is activated and your higher awareness comes alive. You also know that something significant is about to happen.

Yes, when "the call" arrives your spirit is being summoned to answer it. So one day as Robin got off the blue bus and I got off the orange bus I went up to her to begin our "destined" chat…or at least the beginning of our chat…soon other Mystic Travelers joined us and we didn't have the opportunity to really go as deep as we knew we needed to. I remember thinking "ok spirit will arrange for us to have a more extensive talk because there's more…" And as predicted, we were given plenty of time. Our group boarded a lovely train that took us a full day from Cusco to Lake Titicaca. Robin and I found ourselves in the "party car" full of music and good cheer. We found a quiet place in the open air section at the very back of the train. As amazing scenery whizzed by, we soon realized why we both felt so compelled to speak.

In our "spirit designed" moment in time, we realized that we had a number of very similar mystical experiences that needed to be shared. I was stunned to learn that she and I had almost identical experiences in Israel at the Church of the Holy Sepulcher where Jesus was reported to have been hung on the cross. Let me take a moment here to share my experience and you will read about Robin's similar experience in Israel later on in Part II of this book.

While in Jerusalem, I felt a mystical experience coming on when climbing up the stairs to see the cross in the Church of the Holy Sepulcher. In fact before I got to the cross I couldn't move or hear anything. Everything was a blur. It was like I was in another realm. I knew in my gut it wasn't the spot where Jesus was crucified but nevertheless I had the urge, as Robin did, to cry hysterically like I did when I lost my grandmother. I truly cannot explain why I had this reaction but knew it was part of my spiritual journey. Perhaps it was to awaken a memory in me that needed to be remembered so I can more purposively do my latest "spiritual assignment".

In this life, I too can be considered supporting a "spiritual movement" of sorts like the ones of Jesus and his disciples, St. Francis and his order, or those who built the pyramids. Our current spiritual movement is to work with "Conscious Evolutionaries" and "Evolutionary Leaders" to usher in a new way of thinking and being. In order to effectively do that we must all clear our channels and be emotionally authentic. Robin discusses her process to achieving this in Part 1 of the book.

Robin's willingness to be completely open about her mystical experiences is an act of courage. In her travels to almost 40 countries on five continents around the world, Robin has mystical experiences beyond the ones described here. What is so fascinating to me is how Robin and I without realizing it, have been on the same path having similar mystical experiences. For example, here is another experience we had in common.

Like Robin, I also had a mystical encounter with Pachamama (Mother Earth) when a friend and I felt compelled to go to a private section of the grounds in Machu Picchu located on a plateau 8,000 feet above sea level. As soon as I entered the area where all the boulders were, which looked to us like a Peruvian Stonehenge, I felt a state of bliss. It is well known in Incan culture that those who are spiritually attuned can communicate with the rocks. So I was not completely surprised when sitting in front of one of the rocks, my friend and I soon could feel that they had a soul. As they began to communicate with us telepathically letting us know that the energy of what we were experiencing in that moment would always be with us and that we needed to continue our work to help usher in a new consciousness.

The most amazing part for us was the love that we felt from the stones. The heart-energy that they held felt like they were each individuals with a unique personality. We knew that they were part of us and we were part of them and that our connection was beyond space and time. We truly felt honored and deeply blessed that they shared this experience with us. We were overcome with emotion at the gift we were given….to experience first-hand that it is not only humans that have consciousness but as indigenous peoples have told us for many years everything in this world has consciousness. This experience was happening at the same moment that Robin had her telepathic conversation with Pachamama in another part of Machu Picchu. Mystical experiences abound in many places but especially in sacred sites.

To make our experience all the more real, when I arrived back to my hotel room, I found my tour roommate reading a book by a Shaman. I began to tell her of my experience with the rocks at Machu Picchu, she was stunned and said that she just finished reading a line in the book that said, "now you are ready, when you return to Peru the stones of our ancestors will speak to you." That was a double "wow" moment for both of us but we both knew coming to Peru would reveal a great deal for all of the mystic travelers on our tour. As Robin said in her book we need to "suspend our disbelief" because some experiences "just don't have a logical explanation which will satisfy the ego." To many this might be chalked up as one of them.

Our experiences were "out of the box" from the day to day reality for most people but neither my roommate, nor Robin, nor I, nor any of our friends that had similar experiences at Machu Picchu questioned what we each had experienced. No one said I think Diane and Robin had too much sun exposure after hearing our stories. In fact, they were embraced by our fellow travelers as well as ourselves because we knew spirit was creating opportunities and experiences for us to open our awareness to a new way of being. We can live from this place and support others in doing the same. As Robin said "Modern Mystics are anchoring a new way of being." And these types of Mystical Journeys are sort of spiritual training ground for what's possible.

I firmly believe that we are here to help humanity get to the next stage of the conscious evolution. If we are going to get there, we need to join together as Modern Mystics and co-create the present and future we wish to have. We are all here because we have a spiritual assignment on earth. If you don't know what yours is yet, I encourage you to follow the guidance of an amazing Modern Master, Robin Johnson.

Have the courage to tell your story, be authentic with your feelings, sign up for a class with a Modern Master, read as many spiritual books you can get your hands on, go on a sacred journey to an unknown land, join a community of conscious evolutionaries and evolutionary leaders so that together you can "be the change you wish to see in the world."

I have the privilege of working with Modern Masters in the consciousness movement such as our tour leader Gregg Braden as well as Deepak Chopra, Marianne Williamson, Debbie Ford, Jack Canfield, Barbara Marx Hubbard, Jean Houston, Michael Beckwith, Bruce Lipton, Lynne McTaggart, Duane Elgin, James O'Dea, Joan Borysenko, Peter Russell and many others to leverage the extraordinary collective potential of these leaders so that together with conscious evolutionaries around the global we can create a unified field for deeper collaboration and action. This "spiritual assignment" came very clearly to me and I have dedicated this time in my life to it.

It is through this group that I met Gregg Braden and with his encouragement and support I soon found myself in Peru to gain spiritual knowledge that I needed to more deeply activate my life's purpose. And one of the best parts was I had the privilege of meeting a true spiritual sister, Robin and other Mystic Travelers that are also part of this consciousness movement. Perhaps that's why many of us feel so connected to the spirits of Jesus, St. Francis, Dr. Martin Luther King and others that have dedicated their lives to bringing forth a new way of being.

Robin had "the call" to write this amazing book so that you can be at one with the Spirit of God and thus your true nature. Somehow your spirit guided you to this book. That omniscient (all knowing), omnipresent (everywhere) and omnipotent (all powerful) place within is supporting the activation of your mystical side and step by step cleaning out your vessel to prepare you for what's to come.

When you get "the call" as the Nike ad goes "just do it". Your call will be unique to what you need to contribute to the greater whole. Consider it a Spiritual Assignment from God. If your boss at your workplace asked you to take on an assignment would you say…"nah…I don't have the time, resources, etc." Your boss only typically gives you assignments she/he knows you can handle. When you get "the call" your spirit is saying it needs to grow and contribute to the greater whole in a more directed way so surrender and know that you are being guided to access higher dimensions that are available to all of us. There's a reason why you are receiving "the call". Trust that you are here on earth for a purpose and these mystical experiences give us the tools to more deeply activate that purpose.

When Robin had her profound encounter with the spirit of St. Francis in Assisi he said:

"I did my part, now it is up to you to do yours". He then asked her "can you do that, just do your part?" She replied "Yes I can do that".

So ask yourself, now that you are on the mystic's path and activating a deeper alignment with the spirit of God can you more purposively do your part? Since you have all the ingredients to awaken as a chocolate mystic – Go ahead and Make it a Delicious Ride!

Diane Williams
Founder and President
The Source of Synergy Foundation

Preface

It is no accident that you are drawn to read this book. You are on a collision course with your own destiny. As you proceed down your mystic's path, you will discover your destination is bigger and brighter than you could ever have imagined. The only thing standing in your way is you. Yes... you. Your spiritual assignment right now is to clear your channels to allow the Spirit of God to work through you. For those on a mystic's path, in order to be in full alignment with God, you must first have emotional authenticity within yourself. What does that mean? How is that done? It means cleaning out the vessel by being completely honest with yourself about your contribution to the chaos in conflicts you have been engaged in as well as the freedom to express any residual or hidden emotions still within you from the traumatic events in your life.

In Part 1 of "Awakening of a Chocolate Mystic", I describe the bitter traumatic events that happened to me and the principles of life coaching used to reach emotional authenticity. First, I had to recognize that it was necessary for me to master my appetites for the pleasures and addictions of this world and own my bad decisions that led to conflicts. Make no mistake the world is a tempting place. If you have "not" been tempted, then you are not fully expressing all of your humanity and will therefore not express all of your divinity. Divinity comes with a heavy dose of non-judgment which blossoms in its fullness from failures and bad decisions.

Unfortunately, while we are trying to master our appetites for the pleasures of this world, initially we want to keep our failures a secret out of shame and guilt. Does this sound familiar? Have you ever done that? These emotions create room for the ego to hide resulting in a host of other lower level vibrations including: fear, anger, sadness, and victimization that keep us in constant conflict with each other.

Follow me as I openly discuss my bad decisions and indiscretions. Instead of judging me, see yourself in me. Where have you failed? Where have you sinned? Where have you lied? Where have you felt ashamed? Where have you felt victimized? The answers you give yourself are not meant to make you feel badly about yourself. These answers will serve as a light on your path to full emotional authenticity which is a prerequisite for full alignment with God.

I have found that it was not enough to own up to my failures as I learned to master my appetites. It became necessary for me to share my failures and express my feelings with others. Sharing a secret has the effect of bringing a situation to the light which is the only way it gets dispelled. We cannot elevate our consciousness if we are not truly willing to allow our history to become transparent so we can see the nothingness of what we hide. Do you have the courage necessary to share your secrets? For it is our spiritual assignment to become completely clear channels for God's use.

After making tremendous efforts to clear my channels, in Part II of this book, I take you on a sweet mystical adventure around the world. We stop in Greece, Rome, and Egypt before venturing to the Far East to China, Thailand and then on to India only to end a little closer to home in Peru. Along the way, I talk about my mystical adventures which are so unbelievable, even to me.

As I traveled around the world, I found myself initially with more questions than answers. Why is it that I knew my way around some of the world's most sacred sites? Is there really such a thing as reincarnation? Why did all of my mystical adventures involve being connected to the spiritual movement of the time? Initially, my logical mind had real difficulty as it tried to integrate these encounters. Eventually, as the mystical experiences continued to happen, it forced me into a level of acceptance.

In Part III of the book, instead of resisting these mystical experiences, I started using them to help me navigate my current life which has brought me to a whole new way of being. I know longer try to make things happen, set plans, get busy with action steps, instead my life is more free flowing and effortless. My mind is now quiet having resolved issues from my past allowing me to clearly hear the intuitive guidance I get daily from the Spirit of God within. I am happy that I no longer question this guidance which is never wrong, instead I just move from a place of obedience. I laugh daily at myself when I consider what the results would have been had I not listened to the voice of my Spirit. I share this joyful spirit with family, friends and everyone I meet. My heart feels open as I have brought forgiveness to others as well as myself.

Throughout my life, I have come to understand that we are so much more than our indiscretions and bad decisions. We are mystical beings with multi-sensory gifts which are to be used to elevate the frequency of our planet. There is so much to do to bring our planet into "oneness" and make it a place of pure love. Are you doing your part? Read on and see if there is more you can do, not in support of others, but in support of your "Mystic within".

Robin L. Johnson

Acknowledgments

Whenever one undertakes a project of this magnitude, there are many people who play roles large and small. Let me thank all who encouraged and inspired me to share my thoughts with the world.

However, I would like to single out three people without which this project would never have been completed. First, I would like to thank my older sister Pamela Johnson who when I felt discouraged regularly told me to keep going because "people are waiting for this information".

Next I would like to thank Diane Williams who took the time to read the book on two different occasions and offer her expert editing to a struggling writer as she helped me reorganize the book for others to more easily follow. She also graciously contributed the Foreword to the book.

Finally, I would like to thank Debbie Ford, New York Times Best-Selling author for being my friend and mentor in the field of life coaching who emphasized the importance of dealing with your shadow issues.

Special thanks to Danielle Wahab for being on this life's journey with me for the last 20 years and for accepting the challenge to write about her mystical experiences in the Afterword.

I am deeply grateful to my mother Shirley M. Dennis and my younger sister Sherrie Grasty who not only read a draft of the book but also traveled globally with me to witness first-hand some of my mystical experiences.

Gratitude also goes out to: Rachel Levy, Monty Ross, Kristina Hess, Spring Libutti, Madrid Jacobs-Brown, Wadiya Adger, and Philip Peoples for taking time from their busy schedules to read a draft of my book.

I would like to personally thank my international friends Mika Heilmann, Adele Green and Uta Bolduan for their great endorsements.

Special thanks to the ladies of the Expressions Book Club in suburban Philadelphia as they continued to ask me at every meeting, "How is your book coming?"

I want to thank Lynn Diehl of Living Spectrum Reflexology for her energy work to keep my channels open during the two years it took to bring this book project to completion.

In closing, let me thank the staff of Balboa Press for helping to make this dream a reality.

Introduction

"It is time to clean out the vessel" the voice said in such a loud way that I sat straight up in my chair on the patio of my penthouse apartment in Washington, DC. Expecting to see someone, I laughed out loud when no one was there. As I looked out over the Potomac River watching the planes take off at National Airport, I was caught up with the phrase I had just heard, "It is time to clean out the vessel". As I dozed back off in the summer sunshine, I made a mental note of this phrase. Thus, began the "Awakening of a Chocolate Mystic".

Later that day, I was talking to a girlfriend who studied the Christian philosophy of Metaphysics and asked her about this phrase. "What is the vessel?" I asked. Her response floored me when she said, "You fool!" New questions arose within me starting with, "How do I clean out myself?" We talked at length about elevating our consciousness, harmonizing our feeling nature and realigning our belief systems to better hear the "Voice of God" within each of us. I left that conversation thinking that it's time for me to move from my "dial-up" to a "broadband" connection with God or any phrase that you prefer to explain the Divine Source of all life. The year was 1999 with the new millennium fast approaching. Most of America was preparing for the Y2K computer challenge but my focus was on all things spiritual.

Surely, I have not been the only one feeling the need to move towards a spiritual lifestyle which harmonizes everything in my life allowing things to shift that do not seem to be working for me anymore. Like me, are you being pulled at this time to make decisions that seem to make no sense to anyone, not even yourself? Maybe you too are one of the world's "modern mystics"? For years people have spoken of the "Age of Aquarius" as being a time of global oneness, as we experience "love and light". Could that time be now? Could those people be us? No doubt, there is a shift happening in the lives of many of us that we are at a lost to explain.

In my opinion, it is the modern mystics who are anchoring this new way of being. They operate from a place of peace and harmony because they are not in conflict with themselves therefore they are not in conflict with others. They have taken the time to clean out their vessels and channel guidance directly from the Spirit of God. From this way of being, modern mystics are so transparent that it becomes effortless to express the attributes often associated with God such as tolerance, patience, gentleness, open-mindedness, fairness and love. During times of personal crisis, global conflict, or climate changes, could it be the modern mystics in all cultures who stay calm enough to channel in the optimal solutions that benefit the "greater good"? As we move towards 2012 and the uncertainty that is swirling about, how great would it be to have modern mystics able to anchor peace and harmony during those times of uncertainty?

For years, many have written about the attainment of mystical attributes. If you are like me and have read many of the books, you may be a little confused since you seem to be no closer to making your life move with the magic that spiritual connectivity is supposed to bring. What if what was missing was nothing at all? What if the problem with lack of flow in your life has more to do with harmonizing your feeling nature and integrating your life's experiences in order to gain a new perspective which would allow God more room to work through you? In this book, I will share with you, my spiritual journey and the process I took to harmonize my feeling nature and integrate my personal experiences. It is my hope that something I share can support you in accepting the "seemingly unacceptable" on your mystic's journey.

Meaning of Chocolate Mystic

Let's talk for a moment about the name "Chocolate Mystic". Many who know me understand my mystical side. I have always been in search of the "experience of God" which is what mystics are all about. To me mystics are those who seek to effortlessly express the higher vibrations of love while existing in human physicality. We all have our mystical moments when we share information we have no way of knowing claiming "something told me". I believe we are more than just "human with a touch of the divine" we are actually "divine with a touch of human". We all have a mystic within.

As for the word "chocolate" in the title, you might assume that comes from me being a "woman of color". Actually, the word "chocolate" refers to a flavor which takes both bitter and sweet ingredients to make it delicious. In my life, I have had many bitter and sweet moments which make me who I am. So, Part I of the book will cover the highlights of my more bitter moments while Part II covers my sweet mystical experiences. Finally, Part III is bringing it all together in a life that is "delicious". In sharing some of these intimate moments of my life with you, I hope to inspire you to see your own life differently.

Creating a Worldview

Before we move to Part I of the book, let's engage in a short conversation about thought systems that make up our worldview. To me, a worldview is a combination of beliefs, norms, values and experiences that become the filter through which you make decisions. One of the first things required on the mystic's path is the creation of a new worldview that is dominated by God and not by our ego. Thus is the pull that many are now feeling to get involved in spiritual traditions by attending church, temple, synagogues or centers. Grounding oneself in spiritual concepts is necessary in building your faith for your own transformation as well as creating the foundation for forgiveness for faults and frailties in others.

I do not know how it is possible to elevate your consciousness without studying new ways of seeing reality, so reading is a must. Reading and international travel greatly contributed to expanding my worldview. So let me take a moment to explain further. The first book that I read in high school of a spiritual nature was by M. Scott Peck called "A Road Less Travelled". From that time forward, I would read all kinds of books with my favorite topics being: psychology, relationships, inner child work, cognitive behavioral therapy and the world's spiritual traditions.

Just before the start of the year 2000, as part of my mystic's path, I was moved to study religious philosophy starting with the book entitled, "A Course in Miracles". I must confess that after my first reading of the text, it made very little sense to me except the part about the ego. After studying the workbook for one year, it brought more clarity. However, it would take two more readings and another decade of study and life's experiences before I could really understand the new thought system being described.

To me, no study of Christianity is complete without an in-depth study of the Bible. It took me one year, but I read all 1,857 pages of my New King James Version of the Bible. After studying the "official version" of the Bible, I proceeded to look for books on concepts that were supposedly "unofficial versions" left out of the Bible. These readings included: the Nag Hammadi Library, Gnostic Gospels, Gospel of Thomas, Philosophy of The Essenes and debates from the Council of Nicaea meeting 300 years after the death of Jesus to decide what should be in the Bible.

Now that my official and unofficial Bible study had been completed, I was moved to read about the various Christian denominations beginning with the founders of Metaphysics including Ernest Holmes and Charles Fillmore. From all of my readings at that time, the author who had the most influence on my worldview was a writer from the 1950's named Joel Goldsmith. In his book, "Practicing the Presence", we are all encouraged be one with God and to transcend duality, more about that concept later. The study of Christianity took me about three years to complete.

World spiritual traditions were next on my agenda to study for I was looking to see how the concepts in Christianity were similar or different from other religions. Over the next two years, I read sacred books in: Judaism, Islam, Hinduism, Taoism, and Buddhism. I also read the philosophy of Confucius. I completed my study of world spiritual traditions by taking a class on Comparative World Religions. To further ground my understanding, I have visited Cathedrals, Temples, Mosques and Centers in approximately 40 countries around the world where these various religious traditions are practiced.

Over the last 5 years, I have read 120 books on religion, spirituality and even a couple of books on quantum physics and biology. Some of my favorite books include: New Thought for a New Millennium (Michael Maday), Oneness (Rasha) and A Course in Miracles (ACIMI). My desire for learning has also led me to attend many seminars where the "Modern Masters" were presenting their concepts on transformation (see Chapter 6). My process described above is what allowed me to lay new tracks for a new thought system to expand my worldview. What steps are you taking to expand your worldview?

Transcending Duality

Let's continue with more philosophical discussion focusing on thought systems. The book opened with the phrase, "It is time to clean out the vessel". In essence this means moving from a thought system dominated by the "ego" to a way of decision-making guided by the "Spirit of God" within. The successful navigation from one thought system to another can result in the ability to transcend duality and polarity. In our day to day reality we always deal in pairs of opposites which we see as necessary to evaluate the choices at hand.

The need to compare and contrast is a thought system dominated by the ego which needs to judge and weigh each option. This process of decision making frequently eliminates anything that does not fit with our worldview resulting in fragmentation. Much interpersonal conflict follows as we no longer listen to each other while we assign our own meanings to the intentions or behavior of others. It is from this process of decision making that we seek to have lasting relationships. No wonder we have such so much conflict.

In contrast, if one operates from a thought system guided by God, there would be no need for duality or polarity, such as right/wrong or good/bad? From a spiritual perspective, if the Spirit of God is omniscient (all knowing), omnipresent (everywhere) and omnipotent (all powerful) then what opposition is there? In essence, what use is there in analyzing alternative outcomes when the Spirit of God knows all and is leading the decision-making? How great would it be to harmonize our feeling nature and open up our minds to allow the Spirit of God to guide our decision-making to the optimal outcome? For those on a mystic's path, that is exactly what is required of you.

Since it is the thought system of the ego that dominates our reality, planning and goal setting are highly valued. But are you like me tired of all of the striving that comes with goal setting? Are you exhausted from the guilt of falling short of the discipline required to be a "good person" on the road to enlightenment? There must be another path to oneness with God. For at this rate, none of us will ever make it. Could oneness be had by accepting our authentic emotionality for that is how we harmonize our feeling nature? Could oneness be had by "mastering our appetites" for love, sex, drugs, food and alcohol? Could oneness be had by accepting that everyone we encounter is showing us some aspect of ourselves and any changes required are on us, not them? Answering "yes" to all of the above questions was experienced on my mystic's journey.

What I found too often happens is that in pursuit of oneness with God, modern mystics often minimize the importance of their anger and resentment being harbored in their hearts and instead hold to the concept of not showing anger as a sign of enlightenment. In order to be one with

God, the Bible and other spiritual text state that you must first become emotionally authentic with everyone by "loving your brother". Is the lack of being in integrity with your own emotionality slowing your ascent towards oneness?

In order to harmonize your own feeling nature, you cannot get there by downplaying the trauma or hurt you experience at the hands of another. You must fully feel and express any residual emotionality for emotional authenticity is the mystic's path to God. As for me I used the life coaching process which I will talk more about later to access my stuck emotionality. In order to bring this aspect of your emotional expression forward, you should consider talking to a therapist, counselor, life coach, clergy or supportive family member or friend.

Steps on the Mystic's Path

How do we transcend our current worldview to operate beyond our human tendencies? That is what the mystic's journey is all about. I cannot tell you what steps are right for you, but I can share my story and hope it leaves some pointers for your own journey. I firmly believe from my experience that it is possible to get one's ego off of the "starting line-up" of decision-making.

The steps for me required extensive study of spiritual traditions and belief systems in order to create a new thought system which would allow my life to flow effortlessly. Next, I sought a process which allowed me to fully express my residual emotionality which then silenced the chatter in my mind. That process was life coaching which also allowed me to integrate lower level emotions in myself such as guilt, shame, anger, resentment and fear. Finally, to create room for the Spirit of God to operate in my life, I had to master my appetites for the pleasures and addictions of this world.

Without these steps in place, I spent the first half of my life living in "attack mode" where I reacted with hostility to every perceived slight or "potential" for harm. I never understood that there was something in my fundamental belief system or unresolved emotionality that was bringing these experiences into my life. Many will recognize this concept as the Law of Attraction. In short, my way of being before getting on the mystic's path was a recipe for disaster in personal and professional relationships.

This reminds me of a recent dream that I want to briefly share with you. In the dream, I found myself standing in the middle of a forest that had been destroyed by fire. Everywhere I looked in all directions the only thing I could see was smoldering trees and scorched earth. The dream was so disturbing that it woke me up. Unfortunately every time I went back to sleep, I saw the same thing. In the morning, when I finally awoke from a sleepless night, I quickly communed with my Spirit and asked, "What was the meaning of this repetitive dream?" I was told that the "ego is like fire because it is all consuming and leaves total devastation in its wake". I was also told that what I was looking at was the destruction of my life from letting my ego rule. Let's now move to Part I of the book on my "bitter" moments, so you can read more about this in detail.

Part I

Bitter

Chapter 1

Voice of My Spirit

Let's get back to that voice on the patio. I had been engaged in psychology and spiritual study for just a short while and had begun to calm the chatter inside of my mind. This allowed me to hear the "still small voice" from time to time when I allowed it to guide my actions.

However, I have to admit that when I first heard the voice of my Spirit I did not believe it, so I asked my Spirit to prove its existence. Yeah, I will admit it. I did not trust the voice of the Spirit of God within me. I had spent too much of my life in distrust with everything and everyone. I was not going to trust some unknown voice to control my destiny. You see, I am a very analytical person with my rational and logical mind well entrenched. So I needed "proof" if I was to follow another voice taking up residence inside my head.

How did I test the voice of my Spirit you are probably asking by now? It happened on a flight back into DC from Chicago? When the plane landed, the pilot said that because we were early, there was another plane occupying our gate. We were waiting for the air traffic controllers to find us a new gate when my neurotic mind went into overdrive. At this point in my life, I planned out everything to make sure my safety was taken care of. Childhood trauma can do that to you…make you neurotic. Anyway, the many competing voices in my head were debating about whether to take a taxi from the airport, which is always a slow process in DC or take the metro which stopped just blocks from my apartment on the Waterfront in DC, but it was dark.

While this conversation raged inside my head, I heard a voice say, "don't worry, it will be fine". My reaction was "shut-up, I have enough voices inside my head already". The response came, "I am not inside your head… I am your Spirit". My response was "Yeah right". Then I thought, "Wait, if you are not inside my head and you claim to be the Spirit of God within me, then prove it!" The question came, "What do you want me to do?" Umm? What would be a good challenge for the Spirit of God, something I have no way of knowing. I got it, I asked my Spirit to "tell me what gate this plane is going to park?" Since we were not sitting near the terminal gates, I thought this would be a good challenge.

Spirit being the voice of God inside of me would easily know the answer since God in my theology was omnipotent, omniscient and omnipresent. God knows everything without regard to time and space. My Spirit answered my question with the number, "39"… I confirm, "Did you say 39?" My Spirit answered, "Yes". I sat back in my seat with a big smile on my face so confident the voice was wrong. The plane started moving and, since I was sitting up front on the left-side of the aircraft, I got to see the gate numbers as the plane started moving.

As we approached gate 39, I sat up and starred out of the window. The plane started to pass gate 39 and immediately I said to the voice, "See, I never should have listened to you,

you don't know what you are talking about". As I finished my tirade, the plane turned and parked at gate "39"! Now, my whole body started shaking like a leaf in the wind. I then said to my Spirit, "Hey, let me ask you one more thing?" The response was, "no, you just wanted to know if I was real". Woo…woo…did that just happen! The "Chocolate Mystic" has just begun to stir.

Sharing News from My Spirit

In the early stages of hearing my Spirit, I would sometimes doubt the voice and the information given. Here is an example of what I mean. For some reason, my Spirit seemed to have better access to my thought system on an airplane, go figure? Anyway, I was coming back to DC from my family reunion in Las Vegas. The plane was parked on the tarmac in Las Vegas while all the other planes around us were taking off. It was a sunny summer day so there seemed to be no logical reason for us not to take off. Since I was sitting near the window, I gazed out and asked my Spirit "What was causing the delay?" The immediate answer came back, "it was the weather in Chicago" which was this plane's destination.

Sitting next to me in the middle seat was a tall, sandy-blond, middle aged male with the ultimate "Type A" personality impatiently complaining loudly to anyone who would listen about the flight delay. So thinking I was helping him, I decided to share the information I just received from my Spirit. I turned to him and said just as confidently, "the delay is caused by the weather in Chicago". His reaction was very hostile. He said in a very irate voice, "You don't know that"! Shortly after this exchange, the pilot came on the radio and announced there was a sandstorm in the desert near Las Vegas which was delaying our departure but not the other flights. Boy did this set Mr. A "over the top". He turned to me and gave me a quick tongue lashing about me trying to be a forecaster by sharing information I had no way of knowing. I turned and looked out the window with a slight tear in my eye asking my Spirit to clarify what had just happened. The response was still the same, "it is the weather in Chicago".

Eventually, the flight takes off and I fall asleep against the window. When we land in Chicago, there are puddles of water everywhere. The pilot states that all flights in Chicago are delayed because of a thunderstorm that rolled through the area while we were in Las Vegas which has delayed all connecting flights. I doubted the voice of my Spirit, but once again it was right. Now, I could not resist one more round with Mr. A although my Spirit implored me to leave him alone. Instead, I opted to listen to my ego that said, "Get him"! I tapped Mr. A's shoulder as he stood in the aisle in front of me and said "excuse me, can I ask you a question?" He responded "sure". I then flashed a quick smiled as I asked, "If it was not the weather in Chicago, then why are all the planes here delayed?" He looked as if he had just seen a ghost as he went instantly pale. I am sure he was reflecting on the nature of our verbal exchange on the tarmac in Las Vegas. Without answering me; he turned his back and hurriedly deplaned as I laughed to myself.

So why do I share this story at this point? It is to emphasize that when the voice of your Spirit speaks, "it is always right", no matter what the situation is at hand. As they say in Christian theology, don't get caught up in the FEAR "false evidence appearing real". The information being channeled by Spirit is not affected by time or space. The other thing the story illustrates is the difficulty in verbally expressing all messages that are received internally. Not all messages are meant to be shared, especially without invitation from another wanting to know your opinion.

Bumps on the Road to Enlightenment

To me, the purpose of me listening to my Spirit is to be able to bring myself into oneness with God to experience the magic of life that spiritual connectivity brings. However, one of the biggest bumps on the road to enlightenment was my "subtle arrogance" which kept me in the strong grip of my ego. Surely, I am not the only one who experienced this problem. Could this be one of your issues as well? I prided myself on my new found connection with God coupled with my superior intelligence. This lethal combination made me an "arrogant judgmental time bomb" waiting to happen. I was quick to tell everyone how to do everything more efficiently and effectively from my point of view, which of course was right. Problems arose because my "helpfulness" often created conflict with those I sought to help or I felt resentment as they dropped their problems into my lap for me to handle with all of my new found brilliance.

I overstepped an unwritten cardinal rule which states that all Spiritual beings need to respect the "personal sovereignty" of another. What does that mean? It means everybody has the right to choose to live their life in a way that works for them even if it appears that they are struggling. You don't know a person's karmic path or what lessons this life may be showing a person who is experiencing failure on some level? We cannot determine the meaning of life's experiences for another. We can say for most of us that the human experiences of failure and shame are our ingredients for non-judgment. From my study and experience, non-judgment is a perquisite for activating your mystical side.

We cannot judge what another person is doing nor tell someone how to do something for that is the ultimate arrogance. As my older sister Pamela would often say to those she was in conflict with, "Who made you right"? If you, like me have an overwhelming need to "help" someone, chances are you are getting some "emotional payoff". We must take care "not" to impose solutions on the problems of others as opposed to letting them work them out for themselves. If someone wants your help, let them ask and then commune with your Spirit to decide if you are supposed to assist and how.

We all spend far too much time making a mess of our lives then demanding that those who love us fix it. Who has not heard or used the following phrases: "If you love me", "you should", "you must", "you ought", or "you have a responsibility". The situations that we as humans get ourselves into are due to the way we see reality which is limited by our thought system. No one else is responsible for our reality and there is nothing we do can do to permanently shift the reality of another.

In order to correct our distorted perceptions of reality, we must get beyond the things that separate us be it race, gender, nationality, religion, economic status, or history. Many who study New Age philosophy know that the function of the ego in our current thought system is to keep us separate from one another as the needs of the individual supersedes the needs of the collective. As modern mystics, we are going to have to change the worldview that if the collective is considered, somehow the rights of the individual will be overlooked. "Hello", since when is the individual not part of the collective! Therefore, if things are being worked out for the collective that means they are also being worked out in some way for the individual.

Making Peace with Human Faults

As you have read, being on the mystical path does not require you to live a perfect life, but it does require you to make peace with your own human faults and frailties. If you do not, the feelings of guilt and anger which reside within you will be projected onto others in the form of criticism and judgment. We all have experienced failure at controlling our appetites for food, sex, alcohol, or money but ironically, this failure can actually have a positive effect in moving you along the mystic's journey. What you get from these failures is a sense of understanding and compassion for those having the same experience you did. It is easy to judge something you have not experienced, but once experienced your attitude is much different.

Moving towards oneness with God requires an open mind and lack of judgment towards everyone, no matter what the situation. Can you honestly bring that attitude right now? Most of us cannot. We cannot because deep within ourselves we are holding onto some core issues that require a deeper level of forgiveness than we have been willing to give up until now. How do you know if you have not gone deeply enough in your forgiveness process? Simple, if you still react to the same or similar situations that you swear you are so over.

For me, there were deep seated "life patterns" of abandonment, emotional neglect and betrayal which were underpinned by traumatic childhood experiences that were never truly forgiven. This is what held me back from moving along my mystical path until I was exposed to life coaching. Despite reading all of the New Age books I could get my hands on and attending as many seminars as I could finance, a permanent joy and peace still alluded me. I had not accessed my residual emotionality after my traumatic life experiences, therefore could not harmonize my feeling nature.

Life Coaching

Life coaching was the next step that I needed to take to access my stuck emotionality. In 2001 Oprah aired the "Life Makeover" series featuring Cheryl Richardson and Debbie Ford. As I watched the series, I was captivated by the concepts both authors were describing, but it was Debbie Ford that caught my attention. She was teaching from her book, "Dark Side of the Light Chasers" when she explained that many of us are not in touch with the "shadow" aspects of ourselves. This leads us into continued denial of our faults as well as our greatness.

I bought the book and blew through it quickly. By the time I finished it, I realized I had lots of unresolved emotional issues despite the intense philosophical study I had been doing with spiritual and new age reading. Debbie's book introduced me to the concept of projection meaning not wanting to own my negative qualities so I project them onto others by judging their behaviors. To me this concept was mind-blowing. Given my arrogance and connection to my Spirit, I knew I had issues, but not as bad as others, so I thought.

My biggest emotional breakthrough came from participating in Debbie Ford's "The Shadow Process" which is a 3 day weekend seminar designed to allow you to find your shadows. I was so blown away by the process that my life began to change immediately after the seminar. I enjoyed Debbie's approach for working each of us through our own issues.

During the weekend, I had the opportunity to work with Sharon, one of Debbie's life coaches. She was instantly able to show me how my "victimization consciousness" underpinned by feelings of abandonment, emotional neglect and betrayal were attracting to me the very situations I did "not" want to experience. This was the first time I realized that my neurotic need to protect myself physically and emotionally was the exact thought pattern that was bringing harmful and abusive situations to my world. Therein, the Law of Attraction was at work in my life in a negative way. It was my default belief system that was running under all of my new thought philosophy.

When I returned home from the seminar in February, I immediately began addressing certain relationships in my life. Then one by one, people started leaving my life. My business was also negatively affected when I started losing consulting contracts. What was happening to me? I did not anticipate my shifting my beliefs would mean the loss of the world I had created.

By the time the fall came, I was asked to join the life coaching program developed by Debbie Ford. Given all of the changes and failures that had taken place in my life in just a few short months, my response was "I don't think so". I clearly remember having a conversation with Professor Donna who called to see if I was going further into the process of life coaching. I distinctly remember saying, "my entire life is falling apart, and I don't think I want to play with you guys any more". Her response was, "that is wonderful". My reaction was, "Are you kidding me?" Did you hear what I said about my life falling apart? She assured me that I was in the perfect place for all that was happening to me was part of the process of un-concealing my shadows. She continued to explain how I would benefit greatly from the life coaching program which would continue to un-conceal areas of emotional pain so that healing could take place. After a little more discussion, I agreed to take a risk and participate.

Since I was a management consultant by training and running my own business, I always took risks. This was not only an emotional risk, but an economic one as well, for I had to make a decision to sign up for the program before I had all of the money in hand. Since I was in the process of negotiating a contract with an agency in New Orleans; I thought it was a good gamble. Unfortunately, on the day I was supposed to finish contract negotiations, Hurricane Katrina hit. Did I get the message right? Was I supposed to be participating in this transformational training at this time? Have you ever made a decision that appeared to be guided by your Spirit which seemed to initially bring more harm than good? As the life coaching program began, I could not get my homework done. Instead, I sat comatose for several days watching CNN report on the devastation in New Orleans with the inability of our government to assist the millions of people affected in the region. Like others around the world, I was concerned, but my interest was very personal for I did not know the whereabouts of my colleagues who lived in New Orleans. It was only after four days that I got a call from one of my colleagues and was told what happened to everyone that I began to feel relief.

I could now turn my attention to life coaching program. From one of my first assignments, I found that I had many negative programs running in my head. When I did my listing of negative behaviors, beliefs and comments imposed by others, I had six type written pages of negative programming running under my daily four line affirmations. Get the picture. I was so excited to get this information. From my study of psychology the decade before, I realized that I was truly a cognitive behavioral therapist at heart who believed in getting to the root cause of psychological problems in order to resolve them and now I was getting to mine. Anything less than reaching the core of the issue will leave the emotional healing process incomplete.

Over the course of the year, I was able to change my mental programming as well as obtained all of the money I needed to pay for not only that semester, but the next two years of life coaching programs with Debbie Ford. This was my way to emotional wellbeing. I found it was pretty impossible for me to see my own issues and therefore to heal myself. I was taught techniques by Debbie Ford which allowed me to self- diagnosis my own reactions to the behaviors of others.

Now after five years of being involved in the Ford Community and the programs offered, I can honestly say, I am emotionally healthy. The reason I know this is true is because many of the issues that I thought had been resolved by my philosophical and spiritual study came flooding back as I allowed myself to see the shadow aspects of my own behavior. Today, the life patterns that dominated my life bringing traumatic and dramatic situations to my life are no longer occurring.

Chapter 2

Early Trauma

One of the things that shaped my worldview and cemented my ego as the decision-maker was my childhood trauma. As I mentioned earlier, the reason for my neurotic state of mind as an adult was due to childhood experiences shaped by my physical and emotional abandonment and abuse. In my childhood, overall things were good. My mother took good care of me and my two sisters as a single mother in the 1960s. We had the best Christmas children could have receiving all the latest toys including Barbie, Easy Bake Oven, and my dream 3-speed bicycle. We took vacations each summer to the beach.

I lived on a block in Philadelphia that should be awarded the prize for "Living in Utopia" for the way the children played together. Daily, we had community play with approximately 25 children with no adults. The rules were simple, we shared freely with each other and no one was left out. In addition, all arguments and fights were quickly forgotten. I learned to: ride a bike; play softball, handball, and dodge ball; jump rope; play tops; play with jacks; and go sledding all from just stepping outside my back door. I still smile when I think of the good times we had "on the block". Many of those early friendships are still in effect almost 50 years later. I also had great memories of being in elementary school with much support from my teachers. I was always an "A" student and I loved learning.

But it is not the good memories that cause us trauma and lead to the anxious way we live our lives. So let me start first with my abandonment issues. I was a daddy's little girl. As a toddler, I remember my father hugging and kissing me and treating me like a little princess. Then one day, he did not come home. I sat in the big picture window, crying at times day after day waiting for his return. He never came back because he and my mother were divorced when I was 3 years old. I felt so sad and sought out my mother for comfort, but as my mother took on the male roles of sole provider and disciplinarian, I found her emotionally unavailable. Growing up, I don't remember hugs or kisses from my mother who always seemed stressed as she tried to provide for three children as a single parent with no financial help from my absent daddy. So in many ways, my interpretation was that my father abandoned me physically and my mother abandoned me emotionally. I felt very alone even though I had two sisters.

By the time I was 5 years old, I was teased and even terrorized by my older sister who was charged with protecting me. Although my sister swears she protected me from outsiders, her treatment of me bordered on emotional abuse. When I questioned her about why she treated me as she did, she said it was for my own good to make me tough. So with that in mind, almost daily she teased me about being fat, especially whenever I did not give her what I was eating. Favorite names for me were "fatso" or "tub of lard". She teased me when I started school for being smart or wanting to coordinate my school clothes with knee socks.

She teased me for the type of dolls I had especially one she named the "baldheaded Japanese doll" which I refused to give up even though it was hairless. Over the years when the teasing got so bad, I finally would ask my mother for help to control my sister's behavior. Unfortunately, too much bickering by children after a long day's work was often greeted with "handle it" or "don't let me come in there"! The constant teasing by my sister about my weight and other issues began feeding my low sense of self-esteem. I was a little chunky but also very tall for my age but totally out-weighed my older sister. In the absence of my father, I was already becoming an emotional eater. Although parents may not see teasing as a big deal, without the counter part of positive self-esteem, the ego begins to crystallize.

In an effort to feel good about myself, I sought out people who would praise me. I got this positive reinforcement from grandparents and other relatives, but the main source of hugs and kisses came from a teenage male caretaker. The hugs and kisses seemed innocent but I was gradually led into sex. Shortly after the sexual encounters started, I remember one afternoon going into the house to get something. My male caretaker followed me to my bedroom and started demanding sex. When I refused, I remember being forced down to the floor while he raped me. Afterwards, I remember sitting in my bedroom window for hours unable to cry or feel any emotion at all. I was 5 years old. This was the beginning of my ability to "be emotionally gone in 60 seconds" if I felt violated by someone's behavior. I totally withdrew, like a turtle pulling back into a shell. I never spoke to him again no matter how many times I saw him. Many have asked why I did not tell my mother. I did tell her about 40 years later. As a child, I felt that if I didn't "handle it", I would be sent away for creating problems.

It is the experience of childhood trauma that gives us the best opportunity to evolve spiritually if only we are able to bring forgiveness to ourselves and others. We could transcend this density consciousness if we understood that the "essential essence" of who God created us to be remains untouched by these events. Unfortunately, that is not what happens as our worldview of fear and failure crystallize from these early experiences. As for me, I felt that the things that happened to me were somehow always my fault. If only I had been more loveable, considerate, kind or just plain old "perfect", then maybe somehow my life would never have disintegrated into such pain. I no longer trusted anyone who said they "loved" me for those who made the claim of loving me where the ones who caused me the most pain. What I began to seek in relationships was protection and safety; skip the "love thing".

At this early stage in my life, I also anchored a strong belief that "it did not matter what I wanted" since people who were stronger, bigger, older would just take from me. Confirming this belief was the theft from my basement of my favorite possession my 3-speed bicycle that my mother worked so hard to purchase. At this point in my childhood, the message was also sealed, "don't get attached to anything". Soon enough childhood was over, my mother remarried and we moved to the suburbs of Philadelphia for my teenage years.

Making It Through The Teen Years

No matter what stage in life we are in, there is a constant need for support and encouragement. Without that, early childhood trauma gets more and more anchored in our being. This phase of my life goes to highlight that point. Initially, I hated my life in the suburbs. I felt so totally alone and isolated with no real support system except two young adults (local minister and local news reporter). No longer did I have support in school as I found myself the only person of color in the class and often suspected of cheating for having superior grades. I hated that I had moved during my last year of elementary school where I was doing so well they were considering skipping me one grade.

In our new environment, my sisters adjusted much more quickly than I did finding new friends. Instead I stayed in the house the first year in the suburbs and ate "sugary carbohydrates" day and night and night and day, until I had gained 25 pounds in one year! I was very unhappy, but it was nobody's concern but mine. The only good thing that came from sitting home watching television was that I started to watch basketball on television that winter. When the spring came, I got a basketball and began to play. Since I had always been a good athlete learning to play basketball was fairly easy for me and it garnered me some new found friends. However, I still missed my friends from the old neighborhood.

Now the real teen adventures begin. I was 13 and every chance I got to save my lunch money for my trip back to the city excited me. It would take me about 1.5 hours using two buses and a trolley to get "home" to the old neighborhood. Problem was I was supposed to be back in the suburbs by dark. I never made it. I remember one day having gone to the city with my older sister. When we got back, we stood outside of the house and practiced the story we were going to tell my mother when she asked where we had gone. When we entered the house, I told the story we made up. My mother said nothing, just asked for us to tell the story again. This time the story changed a little. My mother would have made a fine attorney as she finally asked for the story again in a very impatient tone. When the "real" story of our whereabouts came out, the punishment was delivered. After a few times of this ritual and punishment to follow because of me running back and forth to the city, I finally came in one evening and told the truth from the start. Result, instant punishment was delivered by my mother. When I asked why, she said the punishment this time was for being disobedient but not for lying….ooohhh. Now I was totally confused. In my mind, I got punished for "lying" and now I am getting punished for telling the "truth". So, my fear of punishment created a belief system of denial. From that point forward, I owned none of my negative actions unless someone could prove that I did what was in question and had the power to deliver punishment. What a warped way of thinking had been created. It is interesting how as parents some actions meant to teach one lesson can somehow create the wrong message.

Throughout my teen years, I continued to bottle- up my emotions which never got fully expressed. My outlet was to release stress through involvement with sports and drugs, smoking marijuana on the weekends in high school. I couldn't smoke during the week because it messed with my grades and my lungs since I was playing basketball. The drug smoking slowly gave way to seeking peace in religion, when I started going to bible study for student athletes. All of these things did nothing to access my blocked emotions which culminated in needing psychotherapy during my senior year of high school which released some of the emotional pressure.

As I graduated from high school, what I did not understand was that my way of viewing reality was completely distorted. I can now understand my neurotic tendencies about my physical safety. As mentioned earlier, the childhood and teenage trauma set in motion in me a pattern of monitoring people's behaviors to get a "jump" on any plans to abandon or abuse me due to their own ego issues. I was constantly now co-creating a reality that sealed in a belief that the world was a dangerous place and I was a victim in constant need of protection. Trauma can really distort reality.

Warped Sense of Responsibility

Another worldview that emerged from my childhood experiences was my warped sense of responsibility. As I mentioned, since my father left and my mother needed support, my sisters and I had to grow up quickly. I can remember in the first years of elementary school doing dishes, laundry and housework. I remember this because the other children were always outside playing while I was doing housework. It was bad enough to have to miss out, but what made it worse was having an older sister who could care less about authority. What this meant was that if she had something else to do, like play outside, that is what she would do. When my mother would come in from work and find something undone, I felt proud that my chores were completed but this shortly turned into resentment. For there were times I was yelled at by my mother for not making sure my sister finished her share of the chores before my mother got home from work.

At this point, without being conscious of it, my sense of responsibility for someone else's behavior is beginning to take root. I spent all of my time until my sister went to college trying to control her behavior. It was done from a very selfish point of view because I did not want to be confronted by my mother for something my sister did. Yes, we all say, we are not responsible for another person's choices, but what happens if your programming from an early age steers you in that direction. Like me, you will then spend the majority of your adult life trying to get people to do what you think they ought to do out of a sense of responsibility.

It took me until my 40th birthday to shed this warped sense of responsibility for my sister's behavior. I remember the event clearly. My mother and sisters traveled with me to Nice on the French Riviera to help me celebrate my 40th birthday. We had not been in the city more than one hour before my older sister said she was going downstairs to smoke. More than one hour passed and she did not return. So my mother told me to go downstairs and check on her. I did not find her smoking in front of the building as she said she would be. When I reported this information to my mother, she was very upset and told me to go back downstairs and "find her"!

When I stepped outside just 2 blocks from the Mediterranean Sea, I could not believe my birthday vacation was turning into monitoring my older sister's behavior. I had no idea where to look, so I started towards the beach looking in the stores as I passed by. Luck was with me because I spotted her within 5 minutes, having a drink and a cigarette while talking to one of the locals in a bar. I went in, told her mother was looking for her and she said "okay" in a minute. When I returned with this information for my mother, she said, "go back downstairs" and get her... now! It was at this point where my sense of responsibility for my sister ended. I clearly remember turning to my mother and saying "no, I am not doing it. If you want her, you go get her. I am done".

Bringing Forgiveness

We have so many dysfunctional family patterns that we continue to hang onto them without realizing their origins. I sometimes think we use this "lack of forgiveness" as a shield to protect ourselves against feeling further hurt. For me, it was by harmonizing my feeling nature through fully expressing my residual and painful emotionality that was the tipping point in my cleaning out my vessel for God's use. Although we may not be responsible for our earlier experiences as children, we can choose to change the interpretation of those experiences as adults. This allows us to bring genuine forgiveness to others by learning to "accept the seemingly unacceptable".

From the pain of my early childhood experiences, I eventually learned to bring forgiveness to both of my parents. Everyone knows parenting is a difficult job that comes without an instruction manual. As a child, I focused on my parents faults and failures, but as an adult, I have now come to understand how truly blessed I have been by what both of my parents provided me.

With regards to my mother, I came to an understanding of her struggles as a single mother and the pressures she was under managing her career and new husband. Despite many demands on her time and resources, it was my mother who was always there for me providing whatever was needed to support my growth and development. I am so appreciative now to understand that the lessons my mother was trying to teach were designed to help me succeed in the "real world".

As to my daddy, I re-established contact with him and his new wife and children during my teen years. As an adult, my daddy and I spent some quality time together. It was during this time that I gave my daddy a "tongue lashing" for leaving me unprotected from rape and not providing for me financially. He also had his opportunity to explain his side of the story. This clearance of emotions between us eventually allowed our relationship to be one of openness and honesty.

With regards to other members of my immediate family, after spending time working through the teasing and lasting imprints on my self-esteem, my older sister and I are now in such sync regarding our views of reality that I nicknamed her the "Banana Mystic". As to my younger sister, we never experienced any emotional trauma because we have always been able to be flexible and supportive of each other. In regards to my step-father, moving me to the suburbs was ultimately the best decision as it allowed me to get a quality education which became the springboard for my future successes. I am eternally grateful for the support he provided during my formative years.

Now as to my teenage male caretaker, that was a tough one. If you were me, would you forgive the person who caused you the most severe emotional damage by rape which greatly contributed to a life of isolation due to trust issues which prevented bonding with others? Well in my moment of truth, I decided I wanted to completely heal my emotional scars, so making contact with him was essential for me. Although 35 years had passed since the childhood incident, I tracked him down through a series of joint friendships. The anxiety in my voice was unbelievable as I spoke directly to him releasing my pent-up anger and outrage. It became easier to forgive him once he sent a letter of apology explaining that he too had been sexually violated as a child. We never know what is happening to someone that makes them do what they do, but we can begin to open our hearts to all people going through life's human experiences.

My mother once said to me, "We all have bitter experiences, but that does not mean we have to become a bitter person". Personally, I found great benefit and freedom from bringing forgiveness to everyone. But I had to do it in the context of my authentic emotionality which helped me eliminate residual anger, sadness and guilt. This means I had to get underneath of the "fake harmony" and stop acting as if everything was okay between me and family members when there were negative emotions still tied up with childhood memories. Without dealing with the residual emotions, my ego continued to hold on to grudges and resentments. But I learned as I released my grudges and resentments, the grip of my ego also released allowing for a new thought system to take hold. In the new thought system, it is the Spirit of God that can now partner with me in managing my new way of being since I no longer hold emotions that separate me from others, especially family. In order to move to a new way of being, we must all be willing to face ourselves bringing an honest review to the patterns of our childhoods to see where genuine forgiveness is still needed.

Chapter 3

Mastering Your Appetites
(Pleasures)

It is not possible to progress on the mystic's path without mastering your appetites for the pleasures of this world including love, sex and, money which are the playground of the ego. In these areas, decisions are made daily which create guilt triggering the ego to respond with fear, anger, resentment and a host of other emotions. It is time to "release the grip of the ego" and master our appetites around our pleasures.

What kind of a person would walk away from a relationship with a smart, handsome, successful Harvard educated attorney knowing that choices of mates at this stage in life were limited? What kind of person would beg for an early out on a $2 million dollar contract leaving $200,000 on the table while having no option for addition income? What kind of person having travelled internationally for 20 years could have no real interest in another international adventure? What kind of person would cease striving for money to buy a bigger house, new BMW, or an improved wardrobe? Answer... A "Chocolate Mystic" who has achieved the goals above set forth by the ego, but found no permanent joy once attained.

Many speak of the power of intention and attention which can help one attain their hearts desires but rarely do people speak of "seeking in any form" is part of the thought system that keeps you striving for more despite the temporary nature of it all. I acquired all of my hearts desires including wonderful intimate relationships, multi-million dollar contract, luxury cars, international trips and a nice home, but the thrill of the achievement was short lived. However, each achievement required constant work to keep it altogether the way "I" created it in order for it to fit into my view of reality.

Unfortunately, the vision I held in my mind of the way "things ought to be" was somehow in conflict with the reality of those participating in my experience. This led to constant conflict and eventual dissolution in personal and professional relationships. I found this to be true with anything I created from a place of desire inside of my thought system dominated by my ego. It took me just minutes to remember many of the spiritual readings which talk about the ego as being about individual satisfaction and preservation.

On the other hand, the greater good can only be found in guidance by the Spirit where everything is provided for everyone. In this worldview, there is no pressure to get others to "do" something or "be" something. Relationships run smoothly as each one freely gives to the other. All of us have experienced these kinds of moments in relationships, but have not been able to hold on to that magic. We experience happiness, but not joy. To me happiness is fleeting and totally dependent on the attainment of some goal. Whereas joy does not depend on anyone or anything, it is an internal feeling that is the normal state of being. However, it is not possible to feel this constant state of joy until you clean out the vessel and master your appetites. So let me share some intimate life stories to give you a better idea of what I mean by mastering your appetites".

Love

There is no greater driving force for the attainment of personal satisfaction than the feeling of love which provides that special feeling that makes all things right with the world. It feels soothing, nurturing, gentle, and protective. What we all give up to have such a feeling brought to us by others. It was during my life coaching program that I was able to see the costs of seeking love outside of myself. During my adult years, as a single woman, I collected girlfriends who were always older and became like big sisters to me in the cities where I lived including Atlanta, DC, and Paris. Since I did not trust people from childhood trauma, I did not have many friends just a few close relationships that I could call on in the middle of the night with "man troubles".

Upon later study, I found a pattern among several of my longer term relationships with my sister friends. I found that I attracted people to my life that were "superficially loving" in that they seemed really caring and concerned but only as long as I gave my total attention to their needs. They also carried a real aggressive side that I believed would soften with some understanding from me. Well 30 years later and thousands of dollars lent to support them did not produce the kind of exchange I was looking for with several of my sister friends. I found out that love is "not" self-sacrifice where every time someone has a need to be critical, aggressive or just downright needy that I should be the one to step in and help no matter what the cost to me.

Let's get into the details of one of my sister friend friendships so you can see what I mean. For over a decade, I had given my sister friend all of the support she needed providing funding when her budget was low, consulting contracts when she was out of work, and spa treatments when she seemed stressed. I even provided the ability for her to tag along on some of my vacations or brought her and her family gifts from my international travels. In short, my failing was that I was trying to "buy love" and the "security" of knowing someone would be there for me.

Over the first couple of years this friendship worked out fine as there seemed to be an equal exchange, but as time went on the relationship became increasingly one-sided. For example, all too often when I needed money, she rarely had it. When I needed to talk, she carried on monologues. When I needed help with projects, she had something else to do. When I needed emotional support, there was always someone else she had to care for. In short, I had made someone a "priority" that only made me an "option".

The straw that broke the camel's back was when I went to my sister friend's city for a conference and she met me for dinner to help celebrate my birthday. She picked me up at the agreed upon time and once we were settled in at a local seafood restaurant, she ordered a lot more food than she could eat. I did not think much about it since she had family at home which would eat it. However, when the bill came, she gave it to me to pay, but she did offer to pay the tip! … It was my birthday but from my sister friend once again I received no card, no gift, no dinner, just a bill.

My mind went immediately to the evening before with a life coaching friend I nicknamed "Angel Buddy". Although I have not known Angel Buddy nearly as long as my sister friend, I also felt emotionally connected to her. When Angel Buddy picked me up the evening before, the first thing she asked was what I needed in my hotel room. When I replied that I needed water, she took me immediately to the store and paid for it. We then proceeded to a nice Italian restaurant for dinner. When the check came Angel Buddy then paid the restaurant bill, gave me a birthday card and even a birthday present. This experience with Angel Buddy was in such stark contrast to what I was now experiencing with my sister friend that something inside me just snapped and in that moment I was "emotionally gone in 60 seconds".

I had felt taken for granted, so I let go and stepped back from the friendship. I knew that I would never again make the concerns of my sister friend a top priority for me.

Unfortunately, it took me 10 years and lots of disappointments to step back from trying to create this "sister girl" friendship into what I wanted it to be. Why so long you might ask? Well, deep in my heart I believed in her and needed her to be like the image I had of her in my mind. From time to time, I would confront her about what I needed. Even though she agreed to change, she could not modify her behavior for long. I am sure many of you can relate to this. So what kind of person would just settle for giving and not receiving equal value in return? What I came to realize in my quiet moments was that I had attracted a person into my life that mirrored my "neediness". So it is no coincidence that I co-created this relationship for it also served to validate my life theme from childhood trauma which says "it doesn't really matter what I want".

When I got to the point where I accepted "neediness" in myself, I could now see and appreciate the friendship for what it was. People who are needy want to use other people's resources (money, time, ideas, and energy) to achieve their objectives because somewhere they are disconnected from the Spirit of God within them which is the true source of all supply. Having an understanding of this spiritual concept allowed me to release the closeness of the friendship without holding on to any anger or bitterness. It is very easy to keep conflict going in these types of unbalanced relationships. We tend to hold on to "potential" instead of dealing with people where they actually are at the moment. We also fail to see what the behavior of the person is showing us about ourselves. As we seek to harmonize our own feeling nature, resolving the residual emotional trauma, we move toward what brings us joy. As we open the door for communion with our inner Spirit, we naturally create new kinds of relationships which nourish and support us.

Sex

For me, the biggest contributors to my promiscuous sexual behavior were guilt and low self-esteem based on childhood sexual trauma. For me, what seemed like mutual attraction with male partners turned into nightmares which were difficult to leave because of the sex. There was no better feeling for me than the intimacy of being held by a man produced intense feelings of being safe and protected. Of all of the appetites to master, this was the most difficult. I will share the highlights of being sexually and emotionally bonded to a man for 20 years but never marrying him.

After college in Atlanta, I met this handsome charming, "I'm all that" kind of man who totally changed my world. He did things the average person his age did not do including taking me to nice restaurants, and even to his wine tastings. On the weekends we took rides out to the mountains to walk the wooded trails. All was just perfect with "Mr. Perfect". Only problem was that one of my older sister friends did not like him nor did her husband. Trust was the main issue always cited by them. I was so in love with him that I did not care what they thought. I was not letting go of this one, especially since the sex was awesome. One day my sister friend's husband asked me to go to lunch and talked to me in detail about the games men play. Since I was just out of college, he thought he would "school" me a little about the "real world". He gave me a series of scenarios men used when dating two or more women, then asked me if any of what he was describing had happened to me. Of course it had, but I always had some kind of excuse to rationalize it away.

Nothing could seem to break this bond that was forming until one day, after a few months of dating my body felt very strange. My pants no longer closed, my stomach seemed upset all of the time. So I decided to take a pregnancy test and sure enough I was pregnant. I couldn't wait to tell my boyfriend that he would be a father. I was so in love with him, I thought he would be glad. I was already seeing my ideal family in my mind. I always wanted to have children, but I was a little old fashion and thought I should have a husband first. So when my boyfriend came to visit I could not wait to share the news.

As he sat down on the floor near the bed, he listened intently to what I had to say about how great the relationship was going and how much I loved him then I lowered the bombshell. When I finished talking, he said nothing for what seemed like eternity. He took his hat off, looked down at the floor and appeared very sad. During this time I could hardly breathe. When he finally looked up, he said, "So what are you going to do"? In an instant my world had collapsed and I could feel the usual disconnection that comes… "Emotionally gone in 60 seconds". I told him not to worry about it, I would get an abortion. He agreed to support me in that. Unfortunately for me, I could not have anticipated the emotional toll this devastating decision would ultimately mean for my life.

After the abortion, there was such a sense of loss I could hardly stand to be in my own body. Nothing I did made me feel any better. I even tried to cling to the boyfriend, but I found out my sister friend was right after all. He had been dating his longtime girlfriend who was back on the scene. I confronted him but he denied it for months. When he finally admitted he was dating both of us, he said he was confused and did not know which one to choose. I told him don't worry about it, I will make the decision.

I packed up my things and within a few months went to graduate school in London. I walked the Thames River every morning before class and cried, then proceeded to get near perfect scores on all of my exams. I sent one letter to him while in London that he never responded to. After I got my Master's Degree, I moved to DC and my sister friend told me that he married his long-time girlfriend. I was sad and disappointed for the love in my heart was still there for him along with unresolved anger and disappointment.

A few years passed before he finds me in DC. We agree to talk and work through a few emotional issues from our time together. I felt tremendous guilt and even more rage around the decision to have an abortion because of his position that it was "not" what he wanted. He said he just wanted to see me happy and that I totally misunderstood his gestures and his comments at that time. He went on to say that he was "not" happily married and is thinking about leaving his wife because I was the "one for him". Ladies, do I need to go further, how many men have used this line and what woman in need has ever had the courage to resist? It took him a few more years of trying, but I finally fell hard for the line that I so desperately needed to believe that I was the one for him. We had an adulterous affair for almost one year while he put his plans in motion for the separation and the sex was off the hook, just like old times. I was over the top with joy, until one day he came to see me and he looked really sad when he got off of the airplane. We sat down immediately and I asked him what was wrong. He said his wife knew there was distance between them so she wanted to go to marriage counseling. I asked him what was his response and he said "He agreed to go". Oh no, here we go again. The first time I took the blame for leaving the relationship but this time he made the decision and both times he chose in favor of his wife.

The strange thing about "true love" is that it stays beyond the sex. Too often, we try to cut people out of our lives when the intimate part of the relationship ends instead of working through the emotion to allow that person his or her own place in our heart. As for me, it took a few months of emotional release of my angry feelings, but in time I found myself in communication with my ex-boyfriend supporting his decisions about his marriage counseling and even taking his wife's side about some of his behavior. What I know is that true love moves you to a place where you want the best for someone, even if that means you may not get what your heart desires for sexual intimacy. For 20 years, I had been chasing a fleeting memory trying to recapture a beautiful experience. Like an elusive butterfly, one does not often succeed. It was not possible to bring the relationship back to where I was because I was no longer who I was. I never had children, I never got married, but I finally was able to take control of my emotions by mastering my sexual appetites.

Money

There are many stories I could tell about how my distorted sense of self allowed me to get wrapped up because of my desires about money. I could tell the story of giving $4,000 to support a friend with an exhibit booth at a New Age conference, only to have the conference unexpected cancelled because of 9/11. Although my sister friend was emotionally upset, she never paid me one cent towards funds I advanced to support her. Or, I could tell the story of helping another sister friend who temporarily separated from her husband, moved to a new city and bought a house. When I moved in to help with the mortgage, I had $2,000 in the bank. However, when I moved out a year later I was $12,000 in debt. To add insult to injury, my sister friend sold the house and made a $25,000 profit. You guessed correctly, if you said I got nothing except for a month after I moved I got back the $600 I paid her for a deposit to rent from her.

However my favorite money story has to do with earning "big money" (millions of dollars). This is where the ego truly resides as many people are destroyed behind "unchecked greed". Everyone dreams of making a million dollars for they feel their life will be wonderful ever after. I dreamt this dream, but what was definitely missing was the belief that this dream was even possible. I remember being in a Ford Institute workshop when Rachel, a therapist and life coach talked to me about becoming an "awesome businesswoman" making millions of dollars. During one of the exercises, Rachel came into my circle and had me mirror to my small group that "I was an awesome businesswoman". I could barely get the words out much less see myself as that, but I am eternally grateful to Rachel for holding that space for my greatness until I could accept that concept in myself.

Over the next few years, my consulting contract awards increased from $100,000 to $400,000. As part of the Secret, I did a "Law of Attraction" exercise writing myself a check for $1 million payable on my birthday in June of 2007. Every day I saw this check as I went to work on my computer in my office and I smiled. When my birthday came in June the desired $1 million did not appear, so I changed the due date to the following year. However by August, I found myself negotiating a contract for $2 million dollars! Yes, I finally made it to the big leagues, all of my money worries would now be over as I was selected with a subcontractor to support victims of Hurricane Katrina in the area of social services.

With big money, comes greed. The first indication of trouble was that I did not listen to my gut instinct about my subcontractor. Although she spoke the language of spirituality, her actions proved she was anything but that when it came to money. Next my shock came with people you think are your friends, they go crazy as well. For example, I tried to get a friend on as a technical consultant, but the subcontractor objected and the funding agency agreed. My friend of 20 years was dropped but then he turned around and sent me an invoice for $90,000 which he said was for money he had to forgo on other projects had he not committed to me. I thought he was kidding and so I did not respond. He then threatened to sue me and I had to get an attorney to settle the case. So the fun with money begins.

I don't need to tell any of you who have earned "big money" about the constant need others have to take what you have. There is this entitlement mindset that comes from others contributing in any way towards your success. It can get really ugly as I found myself fighting over money with everyone involved in the project at some point. Several people were terminated who also threatened to sue. One accepted the termination but did not return company computer laptop. Then there were those who took advantage of unemployment compensation and tagged my insurance even though they were only part-time workers. Finally, the subcontractor who had the ear of the funding agency was able to force me into additional payments despite having a legally binding contract to the contrary.

As far as I was concerned, no one was looking at my side of the equation. As the contract started, I went in a hole for

$150,000 in five months due to advancing funds for startup costs, covering payments of things not covered and being hit with major tax liability for getting first payment from the project on New Year's Eve. For those who don't know, this late payment did not give me time to disburse the income over time, so the federal government was the beneficiary.

As the project moved along, there were constant demands by everyone especially my subcontractor to have things done their way and if not, everyone used the threat of not getting more money as a way to derail the project. Towards the end of the project, I had had enough of the greed that went with the attitudes of entitlement of everyone I worked with. What I wanted more than anything else was "piece of mind". I did not care if the contract was extended. As a matter of fact, I begged for the contract to be ended ahead of schedule even though this request would cost me $200,000 which was to be earned over six months. Money to me was no longer that important. I walked away without knowing where my next contract was coming from or how I was going to earn a living.

What I learned about this experience shocked me. It took several months after this experience for me to see my part in the financial chaos that was my life. I got to see my greed on full display as well as my lack of consideration for the needs of others. I never asked them what they needed to be successful or contribute effectively to the project. During start-up I had all of the answers and wanted to follow my contract to the letter no matter what the reality dictated. I greatly contributed to the fighting as a result of my arrogance and my selfishness. Seeing this is what allowed me to bring forward forgiveness to everyone involved in the project as I began to see their actions in a whole new light. When we master our appetites, it is not always about walking away from a situation, but also about bringing forgiveness and harmonizing our own feeling nature. For the mystic's path requires the willingness to understand all behaviors in self and others.

Chapter 4

Mastering Your Appetites (Addictions)

As we continue our discussion about "mastering your appetites", it is also necessary to master your appetites over your addictions such as drugs, alcohol and food. There are many addictions, but the emotional cause for the continuation of addictions is similar. It is often rooted in low self-esteem and unworthiness. This chapter goes into details about my descent into addictions not for the purpose of condemnation but to make the point that all experiences are ingredients on the mystic's path to enlightenment.

Drugs

Every generation has a drug of choice that act as obstacles on the road to adulthood through which all teenagers must pass. The choice of illegal drugs has been marijuana, cocaine, pills, crack, heroine or any combination of the above. There is scarcely a person alive who has not been exposed to these substances personally or knows of someone who has. The more emotionally damaged a person, the more likely you are to find them at home with illegal substances. My adventure, through the land of illegal substances, definitely had me caught up as a teenager and as a young adult. This is a time in life when you think you are invincible.

As previously mentioned, I smoked "weed" or for all those in the know a "little tweed" (marijuana) during the weekends while in high school. During my college years, I did not do drugs at all. I was hanging around a different group of young people who had wonderful destinies in mind for themselves. Instead of doing drugs, I focused on academics and all those special experiences that would guarantee a good job after college. I spent a summer in DC as an intern with the Department of Energy and had the opportunity to have a private tour of the White House. I spent the fall semester in New York City matching minds with the best and brightest from universities around the country as I participated in a special honors program United Nations semester. I closed out my junior year with a study abroad program in Ghana, West Africa. All was wonderful in my world as I was speeding to the close of a stellar college career tied for 2nd in my graduating class.

Then the bottom fell out. I failed to follow up with job interviews at the placement center until it was too late. I finished college with nothing to look forward to except a short visit to Paris to begin my Master's Degree in international affairs at an English speaking school but not enough money to finish. After this short stay in Paris, I went back to Atlanta but, I could not immediately find a permanent job, so I spent the next year working as a sandwich maker at the local retail chain known as Subway. My sense of who I was at this point was totally shattered. So I was very open when sister friend asked me to try a little cocaine. It was very expensive to buy it, so since I could not afford it, I only "tooted" when offered by a select group of friends.

As time went on some of my friends moved to the New York City area and the fun really picked up. I would meet them in the city and enjoy happy hour, concerts, sporting events which often ended in late nights of endless chatter at a bar while getting high in the bathroom. Since I was in my 20's, I believed I was invincible. You can imagine my surprise when I got a nose bleed from snorting cocaine. The friend I was with at the time laughed and said that was common among "rookies". Hey, I am hanging out with really "cool" people in NYC, I have to show I belong, so I laughed it off.

I did not snort cocaine often so it wasn't until a few months later at a friend's place in suburban New York City that I realized I was in trouble with my drug use. Dazed, I stumbled to the bathroom and started passing out when I got there. I could feel my eyes rolling around in my head as beads of sweat gathered on my forehead. I saw a window in the bathroom and opened it. I tried to inhale as much cold air as my lungs could hold. The outside temperature with the snow covered ground hovered around 12 degrees that night. I remember standing there holding on to the ledge and breathing cold air for an indefinite period of time until I felt stable. When I returned to my seat in the family room by the fireplace, I just politely declined any further drugs. That was it for me forever more. I never mentioned the incident to my friends who were hosting me because they were so high, I am not sure they could have even gotten me to the hospital.

Having gone through the experience of drug usage, I can say I am grateful to have come out alive, literally. Many don't make it out and many others never stop using. I am glad to have had the experience because before it I had definitely strong opinions about those who used such substances. As I often tell people, "it is easy to judge something you have not experienced." Stopping the use of drugs is one aspect of my mastering my appetites when it comes to potentially addictive substances, but learning to not judge others who are engaged in drug usage is a far bigger benefit. What I know today is that transcendence is not possible if one is judging and condemning another person's behavior.

Alcohol

Many people who use drugs also drink alcohol for the same reason they are trying to escape their reality in some way shape or form. But as for me I was learning to drink so I could belong, fit in, feel a sense of community. My only problem was that I had a low tolerance for the taste of alcohol. When I was in my 20s, the love of my life worked at a liquor store so I could get any kind of drink I wanted. So I experimented with wines and champagnes as well as hard liquor. When I started hanging out with my corporate friends, I got introduced to champagne which of course this was the drink of choice for my upscale friends. So at restaurants, I would also drink with them as well as order after dinner coffees with Bailey's, of course. Better times were never had and better memories were never created than restaurant hopping and drinking champagne.

Over time, the amount of alcohol increased as I began to spend more time with my sister friend, her husband and their friends. There was no end to the amount of alcohol that would flow when friends visited with them during the weekends. My sister friend and I have been known to drink as much as six bottles of champagne in four days between just two people. I only did this type of binge drinking on the weekends for a couple of years. I did it for the same reason I did most of the stupid things I did, I wanted to be loved. I wanted to fit in. I wanted to feel protected and looked after.

Although I never drove drunk mainly because I could not afford a car at that time, I was involved in three car accidents with drunk drivers before I began to change my ways. The turning point was the accident that happened as I was driving my sister's blue 4-door Toyota waiting to make a left into my mother's driveway. Without warning, I was rear-ended by a drunk driver traveling a residential street at approximately 40 miles an hour. It is amazing what you experience in these situations. I can remember hearing little pebbles of glass hitting the front windshield as my seat broke sending me flying backwards. At the same time, I felt this blast of cold air as the other car pulled out leaving the trunk smashed into the back seat and the back window totally shattered. The police arrived followed by the ambulance. Although I was walking around, once I complained of neck and head pain I was put on a stretcher and hauled off in the back of the ambulance.

The accident was bad enough but the timing could not have been worse for my mother. There I was in front of her house in a car accident one hour before her mother's funeral. Although the car was "totaled" in the crash, I physically survived with just a bone chip in my neck and permanent injury to one of the disc in my back but emotionally the dangers of drinking and driving were now permanently etched in my mind.

It was easy to forgive my distant elderly cousin whom I had learned was responsible for the accident because I learned that some of the world's most sensitive people consume more than their fair share of alcohol. It is unfortunate that we have created such a world which forces their sensitivities to be hidden in alcohol or drugs. It is also a reality that no matter how much we love someone, we cannot make them stop drinking as long as they have needs which are unmet. As I mastered my appetite for alcohol, I also brought compassion and understanding to my friends who are unable to overcome their addiction to alcohol. Having an understanding of people's limitations is part of the worldview that the mystics experience on their journey towards oneness.

Food

"Are you selling your refrigerator", my neighbor asked? "No, why", was my response. "Because it is empty", he said. A decade after that statement was made, if you open my refrigerator today, you still might see it empty with the exception of a few condiments. The simple reason for this is that I eat mainly fresh fruits, vegetables and seafood which force me to shop every couple of days. It is very interesting the path my food choices have taken. In hindsight, they very much paralleled my spiritual growth without me making an effort to change my diet.

When I was a child I ate everything including red meats until my mother remarried a man who did not eat red meat. I was 11 years old the last time I remember eating any red meat from beef hotdogs to a Philly "Cheese steak Hoagie". Without knowing it, I was already being put on a track for a healthier lifestyle. Over time, since I had a slow digestive system, I would let go of things that did not feel right in my stomach. So one of the first things I let go of in my late teens was soda because the sugars combined with the carbonation totally rocked my stomach whenever I ate food.

In my 20s everything was made of turkey. I could now return to eating hotdogs and hamburgers, but made of turkey of course. I was in seventh heaven as my diet seemed to have lots of variety and seemed to reflect some sense of the normal American diet. I can remember having a conversation with my mother at the time who told me that she does not eat meat every day. I could not imagine that ever being in my future. But by the time I reached my mid-30s, the turkey craze faded as my stomach began to have trouble processing various turkey products leaving me to eat more chicken and fish.

By the time I was in my 40s, one of the first things to go was caffeine. It was a fluke that this happened. I was criticizing my cousin Diane for drinking coffee and smoking cigarettes. She then replied that the five mugs of black tea with cream and sugar that I consumed every day also had caffeine. She invited me to read up on the topic then challenged me to quit drinking tea for one week. So I took her up on the bet, what I did not anticipate was the withdrawal symptoms I would have within the first three days including headaches, night sweats, irritability, trembles. The whole withdraw process scared me so badly it sent me running to the store for any kind of herbal tea which did not include caffeine. To this day, if I am in a restaurant and the only tea available has caffeine this memory of withdraw will flash causing me to decline. By the end of my 40s, I found myself with the inability to process chicken so was left with seafood as my main source of protein that I did "not" eat daily.

As I entered my 50s, a major check of all health indicators showed my health was excellent. I was pleased with my diet with the exception of sugary carbohydrates, breads, cakes, pies and cookies. This was to be my ultimate challenge, mastering my appetites over comfort foods. All of my life, I was an emotional eater. It was the one activity which gave me a sense of control over what was happening in my life. All was well in my world if I had food. After my childhood trauma, I really ate more than my fair share of sugary carbohydrates. I got so chunky that my older sister would tease but that that did not stop my eating. I probably would have been obese if it had not been for my athletic abilities which kept me looking fairly normal even though I weighed a lot.

In trying to control the sugary carbohydrates, I began to monitor my emotional state, but I realized I needed additional support to access what was really going on within me. I took advantage of my participation in the life coaching program to get at some of these issues. Ironically, starting this coaching process on top of starting a new contract resulted in me gaining 25 pounds in under one year. I was so depressed by what was happening to me that I remember buying my favorite pumpkin pie from a local bakery and eating the entire thing in one sitting. I was crying as I was eating, but could not stop. This was the worst case of emotional eating I had ever experienced. Now that I was 50, it was triply hard to release the newly gained weight. After the life coaching program ended and my new contract was moving smoothly releasing much stress, I signed up for a trainer at my local gym. With exercise and some control over my food choices, I lost 20 lbs.

The more time I spent time with myself in the stillness, the more I was able to get a handle on what was happening with me emotionally. I realized that my addiction to sugary carbohydrates is what kept me in the "false glow" or that place of appearing "all was right in my world". Eating sugary carbohydrates produced a high which made me feel good but only temporarily until I ate more. Health studies have shown that this was not my imagination but that sugar affects the serotonin levels in the brain causing one to feel high.

In order for me to break this addiction and master this last appetite, I had to come face to face with the true nature of how I was feeling. I had to become totally authentic with my own emotionally in order to harmonize my feeling nature.

I realized that I had to access the anger and sadness within me. As I began to release these emotions, the cravings began to decrease. What was interesting is that I also found I used sugar when I was feeling good about some accomplishment as well. I soon realized this was my way of prolonging the good feelings of the moments. Is this your issue, do you use food in the same way?

I clearly remember making the decision to cut out sugary carbohydrates by not responding to my cravings. During this period my physical body began to shake just like that of an addict in withdraws. It was doubly hard not to eat sugar just to eliminate the feeling which ironically was caused by eating sugar. In time, the withdrawal symptoms subsided but not before I threw a tantrum, banging on the counter, stamping my feet and crying all over my desire to have sugary carbohydrates. I did not give in but learned to let the feelings pass through me. When my tantrum was finally over, my body felt unbelievably calm. My breathing changed and shifted to a deeper and calmer inhale/exhale pattern. My speech pattern changed as noticed by several people who talked to me. I feel this was possible because this hyperactive energy was no longer running as an undercurrent in my body.

As I continued to master my appetites for food, I began to see that I was caught up in the worldview my ego had created. That is a world of duality- right and wrong, good and bad. As I began to let go of judging everything that was happening to me in these terms, the need to feed the emotions that followed were also released. I started to allow myself to feel the emotionality which over time, this released much of my need to physically feed the emotion. It was not until my father recently died that I truly accessed the sadness within me. Mastering the appetite for food is by far the most difficult because the ego hides easily in our food addictions.

Once eaten, guilt sets in and the ego soon follows criticizing us for eating what we should "not" have. It is from this place of guilt that anger and fear are easy emotions to bear witness to. Oh what a cycle the addiction to food can create.

Mastering Appetites Creates Mystics

The events I shared in Mastering Your Appetites may be shocking and appalling by some standards, but by owning my part in these events, it gives my ego nowhere to hide. Can you be equally as bold by owning your faults, frailties and bad decisions? It is a lot easier to own this human part of yourself, if you know that all of the experiences that you go through in life are necessary ingredients for making you the person you are today.

On our mystic's journey, we keep overlooking one of the fundamental spiritual laws which states that the essential essence of who we are cannot be changed by what we do. This might explain how a person like me who has lived the most common of human experiences is even in consideration for being a "modern mystic". But if you know your spiritual traditions, experiencing the extremes of our humanness is similar to the path that Siddhartha took on his road to enlightenment in becoming the Buddha. One often thinks that mystics are those meeting society's standards of "goodness and morality" as preached in religious orders.

It is my belief that it takes all of our human frailties to open our hearts and minds to God. After our real life encounters with life's failures led by our egos, we can move from a place of "philosophy" about the meaning of something to a place of "knowing" which releases our need to continue striving for some worldly pleasure and maintaining our "illusion of perfection". It is my belief that the "essential essence" of me was never affected by the chaotic experiences involving my physical body. There is something very intangible within all of us that the world can never touch. We are so much more than the collection of our bad decisions.

If we allow ourselves to fully feel the emotions as we go through life's experiences, we will ultimately begin to bring forward the gift of who we truly are behind the frailties. If we are honest with ourselves and authentic in our emotional expression, we are compelled to continue our search for something else…something more…for God. It is our unwillingness to own our stories of human struggle, as I have done here, that allows the ego to continue to have a hiding place.

A funny thing happens as we begin to master our appetites, our mystical side appears and channels open to other multi-sensory abilities such as clairvoyance, clairsentience, clairaudience or telepathy. We all have these gifts; we just need to rediscover them. What abilities are trying to open up for you as a "modern mystic" that you may be ignoring or overlooking? As for me, my experiences have confirmed my clairsentience, the ability to easily feel emotions and vibrations even if not verbally expressed by others. I am also telepathic although I am not sure how it gets turned on sometimes. How do I know these things about myself, it is through my interactions with others.

The first time my mental telepathy was confirmed was while I was visiting my sister friend in Connecticut. She had a house full of company so I was helping her fix breakfast one morning. When everything was done, she asked her father in-law what he wanted to eat. We both heard him say "nothing". So I turned to him and asked, "how about half of everything" and he said, "Okay". So I fixed his plate, put it down in front of him and he ate everything.

While I was doing the dishes with my sister friend she asked me why I had given her father-in-law something to eat. We went through the entire conversation but when I shared what I said to him and his response, she said, "It never happened"! In that instant, I knew some of the other times I was engaged with people I was actually reading their thoughts. In that moment when my mental telepathy is activated, a person will vehemently deny a comment especially if it is of a hostile nature. I have finally had to learn to accept when people say "I never said that" that they were right, they just thought it.

Back to our question, how do we clean out the vessel? From your reading so far of my experiences and philosophy, you can begin to understand what I have been doing for the last 11 years. One of the first things I mentioned was changing my thought system and enlarging my worldview through reading and international travel. Next, I harmonized my feeling nature through life coaching by fully expressing my residual emotionality and accessing my childhood trauma. Then I worked through mastering my appetites for pleasures and addictions. All of this combined allowed me to "still" my mind to be able to hear my Spirit and distinguish it from my ego chatter. This is the background of a Chocolate Mystic. It is important to know that mastering the appetites for me overlapped with some of the initial mystical experiences.

In order to read about my mystical experiences, you will have to suspend your disbelief as I have finally had to do. Some things just do not have a logical explanation which will satisfy the ego. Are you having experiences that defy explanation? I share my experiences here not to compare my life to yours, but to awaken and confirm the mystical experiences you are having are true and serve to realign you with the Spirit of God within. Now, let us now turn to the international adventures which brought forward my mystical adventures underpinning the "Awakening of a Chocolate Mystic".

Part II

Sweet

Chapter 5

Wake-up Call

"Are you still going to help?" asked the man in the brown robe standing over my bed looking down at me. "Yes", I replied. "Well it is time", he said. "Who are you?" I asked. "Francis" he replied. "What does that mean?" I then asked. He answered "Francis of Assisi" and with that the dream was over. I woke up feeling that the conversation was so real and the person I was talking to with the beautiful eyes seemed so alive. What I remembered most was his name, so I jumped out of bed and raced to my computer to see if I could find anyone on the Internet by that name.

St. Francis Is Real

I did a Goggle search but could not find him initially probably because I did not know how to spell "Assisi". I thought he said "Azizi". Since I was not Catholic, nor part of the New Age movement at that time, I had never heard of St. Francis. Once I found information about St. Francis on the internet, my first reaction was "Oh my God, you are a real person". I then called my cousin Vanessa who was a Catholic Scholar to find out how I could get some books on this guy. She told me that since I lived in DC to go over to the bookstore at Catholic University and I would find everything I needed. I made a quick run to the bookstore and picked up four books on St. Francis and my heart began to race with the truth of what I was reading. I loved St. Francis' philosophy of peace and harmony. I felt an instant connection to his message. I resonated with his life story and in parts knew what was going to happen even before it was addressed in the books, which I found rather odd but shook it off.

After reading about St. Francis, I felt honored to have had this dream, but what was it that I had agreed to do? Was I somehow to continue to share his messages with the world? Was I to become a Franciscan Nun? I had no idea, but what I did know was that this qualified as a "mystical experience" since it could be verified that St. Francis was real. At this time in my life, I was probably the most practical, logical, analytical, left brain person you would ever want to meet. So although I had this mystical experience, at first I did not put much stock in it. I found it an interesting experience to ponder what was possible in this dimension of reality but only time would show that this mystical experience was so much more.

World of Consulting

The vision of St. Francis came to me at dawn of the new millennium in the year 2000. By the spring of that year, my life was beginning to take a turn for the worse. As a management consultant, it was time to renew my contract. There was an agency which asked me to provide additional consulting services for public private sector partnerships. Since I was a subcontractor, I shared this information with the prime contractor who was excited because it meant additional funds would be forthcoming. When it came time to sign a new contract, there was a lot of language in the contract which I felt took away my rights on the public private economic model I was developing which made me hesitate in signing the agreement. So I hesitated in signing the new contract.

One night during this negotiation process, I had a dream that I was walking up one of the mountain roads of the French Riviera. The prime contractors told me to just "come on" as they rounded the corner out of sight. In the dream, I remember looking out over the blue water of the Mediterranean Sea thinking how beautiful it was. Instead of following the contractors as I was supposed to do, I found myself going off the cliff towards the water. But since it was a dream, I did not fall but floated as angels with wings came to me saying things like "glad you came", "we have been waiting for you" and other wonderful messages.

So when I woke up, I decided that it must have been a message from my Spirit, so I cancelled the renewal of my contract. Needless to say, in my arrogance I never stopped to check with my Spirit which proved to be an important lesson going forward. No sooner did I announce to other agencies that I was available for the projects they recruited me for, not one of the other contracts materialized. Now here it is approaching the summer of 2000 and I am without a job with car note and rent to pay. I finally got a short contract with an agency, but within a few months it too was cancelled. I did not panic at first, for I thought it was all part of some big mystical experience that would soon end.

Communing With Spirit

During this hiatus, I spent the nights reading religious books and praying to the Spirit of God within me for some clarity about my life as I tried to move my life in a new direction. I remember fasting for days at a time. I was losing weight as I was eating less while walking or riding my bicycle along the Potomac River. The nights blended with the days as my sleeping pattern morphed into naps in the afternoons and up before dawn. I was feeling good as I continued having my conversations with the Spirit of God in me and I felt the trust was growing.

One day, I was reading in the Bible about the concept of "man being made in the image of God". So I asked my Spirit what that meant. The answer was, "go make a cup of tea". Given my rambunctious nature, my reply was "what does that have to do with my question"? As the water started to boil and steam was coming out of the tea kettle, my Spirit said that the image of God in man is more like steam in its formless nature rather than looking like a physical body. So I tried to capture the steam by grabbing at it or smothering it and the essence of the steam could not be controlled. No matter what I did, the steam escaped through my fingers as I tried everything to capture it until I broke out laughing. So for me, when clergy say that man is made in the image of God I laugh as I think about steam.

Financial Chaos

Well the laughter and freedom I was experiencing began to turn to worry and dread as the weeks without money, now stretched into months and the months were now approaching one year. I was now at the end of my savings and had blown through every credit card some institution gave me. What am I supposed to do now? The bottom started to fall out when my monthly rent of $1,600 was due on my DC penthouse apartment but I did not have it. I was waiting for a lump payment from work completed on a previous contract, but the funding never came.

In the meantime, I got a white slip from the courts regarding my upcoming eviction from my apartment. The notice requested that I appear in court regarding my lack of payment on the rental property. I continued to pray and asked for guidance, but nothing. I remember after I got the next notice regarding the eviction, this time it was yellow, I started making demands of this new God to fix this situation. Finally, I remember standing in the living room looking out the patio window at the Washington Monument saying to myself, "if I have to give all of this up, it is okay because I am too far in not to trust my Spirit now". If this is some sort of test of faith, then I will allow whatever is to come to come. I went to sleep fairly calm.

The next day the pink slip for eviction appeared, the court hearing was the following day. I went out did some grocery shopping, stopped by the mailbox on my way back in and froze in my tracks. The check that I had been waiting for was in the mailbox. The total amount was $25,000. Needless to say, I did not have to move. It took another six months to get with another consulting company on a multi-year contract but that was okay with me.

Miracles In Sedona

As the fall of 2001 approached, I decided to go with my sister friend to Sedona, AZ. I had heard a lot about the place now that I was tuning into spiritual literature. I thought it would be fun to visit and do a side trip to the Grand Canyon. I was totally open to whatever the experience would bring with no expectations. Once we arrived in Sedona, it did not take long to find our way around town and to locate the vortexes of energy that the locals speak about. Several days into the trip, we decide to do some "other worldly" adventures by going to a psychic reader to learn about our future destinies. My girlfriend came out all excited about the vision she had been given, now it was my turn.

When I walked into the room, there were 12 pictures of very wise looking elders on the wall. I asked who these people were and the answer she gave was "ascended masters". I told her I had never heard of the term before as I continued to look at the pictures. I finally asked her about a specific picture that I was drawn to. "Who is this guy" I asked? The answer was Kuthumi. Don't know why I asked, I had never heard of him either. So we began the reading about my destiny. It took very little time to establish the connection between me and St. Francis. She told me that Kuthumi is reported to have worked with the energy of Jesus and St. Francis.

After my reading was over, the psychic reader sent me around the corner to an oil shop to get the fragrance associated with Kuthumi so I could channel in messages better from St. Francis. I said I would do it as I took down the address. My girlfriend and I went to the oil shop and I told the owner what I was sent there for. She said okay, but first you must look at these various colors of liquid containers and let me know which one you are drawn to. After about a minute, I picked one with a yellow glow and she looked at the label under it. She picked up a book, looked up the number associated with the colored liquid and told me to read that section then come back to her. I thought this was weird, but okay, hey this is Sedona.

As I made myself comfortable, I began reading about the yellow liquid with the corresponding number. Within a few lines of the paragraph, the sentence said that this color yellow is associated with Ascended Master Kuthumi and St. Francis! What? Get out of here… I reread that section several times. My mind was totally blown. I bought the essential oil from the shop in Sedona, but did not leave the city until I also purchased a 3 foot high statute of St. Francis as well. I am now convinced that my "wake- up call" at the beginning of the new millennium was real. I know the existence of St. Francis is real. Now this trip to Sedona totally confirmed my connection to St. Francis is also real. But the question still remained, what is it I am supposed to do?

Chapter 6

Encounters with Modern Masters

For thousands of years, every civilization has had people who provided philosophical or spiritual wisdom to help alleviate the chaos and conflict that appeared in people's lives. Greece had Plato and Socrates among others. Asia had Lao-tzu, Siddhartha (Buddha), and Confucius to name a few. Today in the West, we have what I call our Modern Masters of the New Age movement which include names like Louise Hay, Barbara Marx Hubbard, Ram Dass, Eckhart Tolle, Dr. Wayne Dyer, Caroline Myss, and many more. My library includes 120 books by these Modern Masters.

We are so fortunate to live in an age when it is not only possible to read these inspirational writings, but we also have the ability to see these Modern Masters at conferences put on by groups like Omega Institute or Mishka Productions. During my mystic journey, I have taken advantage of these opportunities by attending lectures with the following Modern Masters: Debbie Ford, Dr. Wayne Dyer, Cheryl Richardson, Iyanla Vansant, Rev. Michael Beckwith, Marianne Williamson, Gary Zukav, Deepak Chopra, Caroline Myss, James Twyman, Neale Donald Walsh,

Gregg Braden, Dr. Brian Weiss, James Van Praag, Byron Katie, Mark Victor Hansen, Arielle Ford, Joan Borysenko and Abraham (Esther/Jerry Hicks).

On the road to enlightenment, we need much support for what we think we understand. After reading the books of the Modern Masters, we sometimes discover we really do not completely understand the concept, so there is nothing better than a live conversation with the author where these concepts are further discussed. The Modern Masters with the level of spiritual work that they have done on themselves are constantly modeling a "new way of being". They freely engage us in an emotionally authentic and joyful way. During their lectures, they demonstrate the importance of staying connected to their Spirits to deliver the messages meant for us. These Modern Masters not only provide inspiration and encouragement, but many of them have training programs which allow us to further explore our own paths. The new world that many of us are drawn to create requires that we belong to a new type of community which the Modern Masters offer.

Long Reach of Modern Masters

With that being said, let's talk about how the Modern Masters have personally impacted my life during my mystical journey. My most recent experience happened during the spring of 2008 while in India assisting with a workshop based on the work of Debbie Ford. After the conference on "Sacred Feminine Energy" was over, I stayed almost another week in India. I left the city of Jaipur and went back to a Westin Hotel and Resort outside of New Delhi. After resting sufficiently, I hired a driver and took off for the Taj Mahal in the city of Agra as suggested by my younger sister Sherrie. The day was simply splendid as I took in the Taj Mahal and additional sites around the city of Agra.

When it came time to leave the city, my guide decided now it was time to shop. My first stop was the carpet shop where I had no intention of buying a carpet to lug home, but I did. Next, I went to the marble craft shop to see how the details of the Taj Mahal were created. Samples were shown which I did not need to buy, but I did. Finally, I asked the guide to take me back to the hotel in New Delhi but he replied just one more stop by the jewelry store. Okay last stop I agreed. Since the prices were escalating as we went to each shop, I was determined to make this stop quick.

As I descended three steps to enter the small shop, the owner was very gregarious and seemed genuinely happy to see me. I looked at the beautiful jewelry he had for sale and told him I was not really interested. So he began a conversation with me like the usual tourist talk…Where you from? How long you been here? Do you like India? Then he asked a surprising series of questions, "Who are you? Are you someone famous?" By this time, I am truly cracking up thinking "oh my God, what a sales pitch"!

As the conversation continued, he said there is something about your energy field, "you are somebody important", and you can tell me; I will keep your confidence. I thought about what he said for a moment before I laughed even harder. Then the long reach of the Modern Masters showed up when he asked me, "Are you one of Michael's people"? Who are you referring to? I asked. His response, "You know Rev. Michael Beckwith, the minster of Agape International Center in Los Angeles and the man in the movie "The Secret". I told him I did not personally know Rev. Beckwith, but was scheduled to see him present at the Omega Institute's conference in New York in a few months. He said, I knew it, you are one of them. I can tell you meditate often, I can see it in your aura field.

I changed the subject and asked him how he knew of Rev. Beckwith. He replied that he hosted him and his delegation during the special meditation sessions Rev. Beckwith held at the Taj Mahal. As I left with some small earrings and a statute of Shiva that I did not need, he said, when you meet up with Michael, tell him Smitty said "hi".

Well the story should end there, but it did not. I did see Rev. Beckwith in New York, but did not have time to share the story. However as fate would have it, I met him that fall as he was presenting on the Bob Proctor cruise of the Caribbean. Even though I did not know Rev. Beckwith personally, I saw him in the cafeteria and shared this story with him. He seemed genuinely entertained by my encounter with his friend "Smitty" in India. This story illustrates not only the long reach of the Modern Masters, but also how approachable the Modern Masters can be in public places.

Enlightenment at Omega

One of the ways I get to see many Modern Masters was by attending conferences where many of them were lecturing. In the fall of 2004, I took advantage of the opportunity to see many of my favorite Modern Masters all in one place as the Omega Institute held its conference in Miami, FL. During the conference, one of the first presenters I was privileged to see was Debbie Ford whom I had seen on Oprah with Cheryl Richardson a few years before. Watching her live, I loved Debbie Ford's energy and authenticity from the moment I heard her speak. So when she finished, I was one of many people who jumped in line to get my book signed by her. It was her classic book entitled, "Dark Side of the Light Chasers". When she got to me, she was very friendly and with a big smile asked me my name. While she was autographing my book I was telling her how much I enjoyed reading it and how much it changed my life. She looked up at me and said, "You would make a great life coach in my program". I replied, "I don't think so because I read your book and I have too many issues". She replied, "You are just the kind of person we need". Here is the number, call my guy Jeff. My head was buzzing from the conversation as I tucked the number away and continued on with my adventure at Omega.

It was really Dr. Wayne Dyer who drew me to the Omega Institute Conference that year. I had been watching him for years on public television and was one of Dr. Dyer's biggest fans. I think I purchased every book he wrote for almost 10 years. In my library I have some of his classics including "Erroneous Zones", "You'll See It When You Believe It", "Real Magic", and "Your Sacred Self". However, it was his book entitled "Spiritual Solutions to Every Problem" that motivated me to meet Dr. Dyer. From reading that book, I realized there was a connection Dr. Dyer also had to St. Francis. I also noticed a shift in his subject matter from psychology to spirituality. What was fascinating to me was that Dr. Dyer's shift towards spirituality mirrored my own. After Dr. Dyer's lecture, he was signing books so once again I took that opportunity to talk to him briefly about increasing my connectivity to St. Francis. Dr. Dyer suggested I go to San Francisco and meditate at the Grace Cathedral and walk the labyrinth. I told him I had already done that a few times. So he said that I should go to Assisi that would be my next stop. I thanked him and as I walked away I thought to myself, maybe someday I will. But since, I had recently taken the usual tourist trip to Italy, I wasn't feeling all that moved.

The next session was with Dr. Brian Weiss on the topic of past life regression. As the session started, Dr. Weiss introduced two women from Italy who were sharing his work in Italy. As for the format of the session, Dr. Weiss announced that he would conduct a short regression session for those interested in participating. So I jumped at the chance and got down on the floor and started to relax. Fresh on my mind was my discussion with Dr. Dyer, so I thought I would see if I could take myself on a quick trip to Assisi! As the regression session started, it was difficult keeping Assisi in my mind. Since I had never been there, I could not visualize it. Then like a dream as I relaxed, I saw myself in this walled medieval city on the side of a hill with limestone colored buildings. I was dressed like a monk in the usual brown robe, but it was rough like a sack cloth used to carry potatoes.

As the vision continued, I began to feel emotionally sad as tears starting falling down my cheeks. What I was seeing was the way the first monks of St. Francis were treated as they begged for food from the well-dressed people. During that time being the 12th century in Italy, people often wore clothes of silks and satins reminding me of Christopher Columbus. But it was not their clothes that caught my attention, but their attitudes. In the vision, they looked down on the monks very much the same way as we look down on homeless people today.

The vision was now feeling more real than ever so I took the opportunity in the vision to ask a fellow monk to take me to St. Francis which he promptly did. Unfortunately, I cannot remember the details of the conversation as we descended some church steps. What I do remember is seeing St. Francis at the end of his life dying in what looked to me like a cave with a rounded ceiling and light stone walls.

When I awoke from this regression session, I was blown away by the feeling and the reality of what I had just experienced. Even though Dr. Weiss was sharing some information, I could not internalize any of what he was saying for my attention was on someone to corroborate or dispel my story and quickly. As Dr. Weiss closed, I moved swiftly towards the stage and asked Dr. Weiss to get the women from Italy to come down front to chat with me. When they arrived, I told them what I had seen in my vision describing the city of Assisi perfectly with its white limestone looking walls. I also described the attitudes of the people of that time towards the monks. The women listened very attentively and when I finished both said that everything I saw was true. My head was really spinning out of control now. You could say I was experiencing enlightenment at Omega.

As soon as I left the room, I called my travel agent and told her what had just happened to me in my regression session and told her I wanted to participate in her upcoming trip to Italy with a special trip arranged to visit Assisi. I then called my mother, told her what happened and asked her to go with me to Assisi. Although she had already been to Italy as well, she agreed to go back with me. It was now time to meet St. Francis.

Chapter 7

Rendezvous with St. Francis

Our trip to Italy during the spring of 2005 came at a highly spiritual time because as we landed in Venice, Pope John Paul II was gravely ill. Many of the Catholic faithful from around the world had descended on the Vatican to pray for the Pope. The vigil lasted a few days before Pope John Paul II died and a successor was to be chosen. For those of us who were not Catholic, we found ourselves also praying hard that the closed door meetings would produce some white smoke soon indicating a new Pope had been chosen. We watched the news in Italian daily especially as we moved from Venice to Florence then finally to Rome. Our concern as tourist was that we had paid for a group tour of the Sistine Chapel which was closed until a new Pope was chosen.

Fortunately for us, a new Pope was chosen by Friday so early Saturday morning, we were having our tour of the Vatican sites including St. Paul's Cathedral and the Sistine Chapel. As my mother and I walked through the square, we could see all of the construction for the installation of the new Pope. While close to a million people were expected in Rome over the next few days, my mother and I were heading out of Rome towards Assisi. Finally, the purpose of my trip was at hand.

As we travelled though the rolling hills of the Italian countryside, I wondered what I would see. Up to this point, I did not believe in reincarnation but now the door was cracked open for that concept to be a reality for me. I pressed my face to the glass of the train window looking intently at every little village we passed. Finally, after a couple of hours on the train, I saw it, a city on the side of the hill surrounded by a white limestone looking wall. I was so excited. After we dropped our bags at the hotel we headed straight for the walled city.

St. Francis Speaks

When we reached the top of the hill, I did all I could to not run up through the gates. When I was finally able to get close enough, I just touched the walls and sighed, "I can't believe it" for the color of the walls looked just like they did in my past life regression session with Dr. Weiss. I was at a loss to explain this. At a time like this, there are no words. The feeling was magical. I could not stop smiling as I looked around following the crowd into a large church. Since my mother and I had travelled to most of the European capitals, we always took time to visit the main Cathedrals and light candles. So this made a lot of sense that visiting this church would be our first stop.

After we took a short tour of the church we followed the crowd towards a narrow set of steps. As we descended in single file, we realized that we had now entered the grotto where they kept the remains of St. Francis. There was a sign posted that said, "Silence". People walked single file past the few pews towards this golden monument at the center of this small chapel. There was room to walk completely around the monument then proceed towards the exit. As we joined the slow silent procession, my joy was beginning to fade and became replaced with a somber feeling. With each step closer to the monument of where the remains of St. Francis were buried, the weaker my knees became. Just as we were passing the remains, I felt so weak I could not walk any further. I told my mother I had to sit down immediately.

As I stared at the golden monument for a moment, the tears began to fall, slowly at first, then fast and furious. I was crying as hard as I would at the loss of my mother or father. I could not stop the deep felt emotion that was coming up from within me. The harder I cried, the more emotion was released then all of a sudden the sadness was replaced by intense anger. In the middle of this crying spell, in my mind, I started telling St. Francis off! I remember saying something like, "You wasted my time when I followed you. You said things would be better. It has been 800 years and we still have war and poverty. Nothing has really changed." That is when I heard it, the same voice that had awakened me at the beginning of the new millennium.

The voice of St. Francis said to me, "Antonio, you are still the same". My response to that was, "What are you talking about"? St. Francis went on to say, "You were impatient then and you are impatient now". The rest of the conversation was about me spending too much time being the "morality police" making sure everyone was "doing the right thing". In my quest to control the behavior of others, I completely missed what St. Francis was trying to do. My question then was "What was that"?

St. Francis explained that too many people of medieval times had become so materialistic that they had moved away from the "message of love" taught by Jesus. St. Francis went on to say that he was simply creating another way for people to find their way out of those values and realign with God because there is a difference between morality and love. Morality is based in judgment where love is based in tolerance.

St. Francis then said "Be quiet and listen". For what, I thought? All I heard were the shuffling of feet across a concrete floor, this endless movement. St. Francis said, "We were successful because people are still coming because they believed in what we taught". When he was in the world, St. Francis said, "I did my part, now it is up to you to do yours". He then asked me "can you do that, just do your part?" I replied, "Yes I can do that". At that moment, my telepathic conversation was over as my mother tugged on my jacket and said we have got to get out of here because people are looking at you kind of crazy. What I did not realize was during this telepathic conversation, I was moving my head up and down just as if I were having a real discussion with someone.

Knowing My Way Around

After we left the church, I told my mother what St. Francis had said and in particular the line about "just doing my part". My mother listened patiently then said, "Okay, let's find a store in the City of Assisi where I will buy you something to remember this trip". As we moved through the town, it was weird but all kinds of memories flooded back. I could see fountains with no water suddenly flowing with water and knowing that is how we gathered water daily during the times of St. Francis. I could look up or down alleyways and instantly know where the road would lead. We finally popped into one store and my mother purchased for me a white stone carving of St. Francis.

Since my mother was starting to get tired, so she wanted to return to the hotel. I quickly told her, no problem, we can go down these stairs here and this will lead to another road which will take us back out. Are you willing to try it?

She laughed and said "why not"? Off we went and of course my directions were flawless as we moved along a quiet street with very few tourists towards the front gate. Wow, what an experience. I could hardly contain my excitement from the activities of the day.

Back at the hotel, as my mother watched the television about the installation of the new Pope, I read the literature I had picked up at the church. It talked about the life of St. Francis and then I saw it in black and white. The quote said, "When St. Francis died, he is reportedly to have said, I did my part, now it is up to you to do yours". I read it to my mother and she just stared at me. In my mind, I am now a true believer when it comes to reincarnation, but there is one part of the story that still does not fit for me. I still need to see the place where St. Francis died. In the regression session, it looked like a cave to me with a rounded ceiling.

Right and Wrong

The next morning, we set out to find the place where St. Francis died. We went to the local church outside of the walled city. As we entered, we learned that the new church surrounded part of the ruins of a much older church. I was told by the guides that St. Francis died there. "No...no way that could be the place" I thought. I remembered from my regression session not being able to stand completely up in the place where St. Francis was dying because it had rounded ceilings like being in a cave. Maybe I got this part of the story wrong, so for the sake of it, I thought I would just take a quick peek at the place they claimed St. Francis died.

When I looked through the window of the original church, my heart skipped a beat and my breathing went completely shallow. In that moment, I was both right and wrong. St. Francis did not die in a cave like I had seen in my regression session, but in the storage facility of a church. As I stood there and stared, I saw the rounded ceiling and light stone walls just like in my vision. It was real, all of what I saw. I am standing here looking at it with my knees shaking and chills running through me. As I walked away, I knew I was now forever changed. I had officially reconnected to "Ces" nickname for Francesco. Now having experienced this, I know that all things are possible on a mystic's journey.

Chapter 8

Ancient World

Much is written about the Ancient World, the great civilizations created by the Romans, Greeks and Turks that ruled the Mediterranean region at one time or another. Having been to Rome, it was out of natural curiosity that I set out to explore the other countries around the Mediterranean. Greece was next because while on tour in Rome, I often heard the expression, we were inspired by the Greeks with this design.

Greece – City of Corinth

In the spring of 2006 I did not go to Greece in search of a mystical experience, I went because I wanted to continue exploring the world. Even though I had a mystical experience in Italy, it never dawned on me that I would have other mystical experiences. Funny thing about mystical experiences, once you are open to concepts like reincarnation, then anything is possible. When my family and I landed in Athens, we were struck by the beauty of the city. On the road to downtown, you could see these rolling hills with these white washed apartment buildings in what appeared to be a semi-arid climate. There was not a lot of grass or tall trees like we are used to seeing in Philadelphia.

Once we checked into the hotel, we had a quick meeting with our group before heading to our hotel room. Given that my family and I have traveled internationally several times before, we implemented our "international travel rule" which states that we must go to bed immediately no matter how we feel, so we can get back up the same day to get on local time as soon as possible. We slept peacefully in the beautiful hotel for hours before getting back up to visit the shops that surrounded the bottom of the Parthenon. As I looked up to see the Parthenon which was a giant complex of Temples on the hill, I could not believe I was walking around in Greece. This is the land of philosophy and mythology which forms the basis of much of Western Civilization, not to mention they also had great food.

Since I had done my fair share of Bible study, I made arrangements to travel to the ancient city of Corinth about 50 miles outside of Athens. This was one of the cities in the Bible where the Apostle Paul, a contemporary of Jesus, spent time trying to spread Christianity. Although Paul spent some time in Athens around the Parthenon, according to our guide, Paul's spiritual arguments failed to convert the intellectuals of that time who were students of the 350 year old philosophies of Plato, Socrates and Aristotle. As a result, of not making many inroads in Athens, Paul created a base in the influential city of Corinth which at the time of his arrival was already 600 years old.

To get to Corinth, we hired a local taxi. I was so excited to be able to have the Bible site come alive, little did I know what was really motivating my excitement. When we arrived in Corinth, the driver took us to the back of the city near ruins of the old amphitheater that at one time seated 10,000. After visiting a museum that was open, we wondered through the ruins of the City of Corinth. We stopped first at a Temple with just a few remaining pillars before continuing on our walk through the ruins. Then I saw it and said to my younger sister with excitement, "there's the fountain"! She replied "What, that pile of rocks?" She then opened her map and it said "fountain".

At that moment, some basic memories came flooding back to me as I pointed out the main street with many of the white marble slabs still in place. I also said with great confidence that what is now the "exit" was really the entrance to the city as proof I offered the placement of the Roman Baths. In ancient times, many travelers upon entering a city would stop off at the bathhouses first so they were always near the gates of the city. As we left Corinth that day, I felt really happy but a little puzzled about how I knew so much about that city. I can't say I gave it much more thought as we continued our tour of the Greek Isles. I loved the ports of call including Mykonos, Rhodes, Santorini, Patmos and Crete.

What is interesting is that places I would have thought would lend themselves to mystical experiences did not. For instance, the island of Patmos is where John was imprisoned by the Romans. It is said that this is where he wrote the final chapter of the Bible entitled the "Book of Revelations". While touring the area where John was imprisoned one would think this is an ideal place for a mystical experience, but I got "nothing"... zip, nada, nil. From this I have come to realize, mystical experiences are not something you can conjure up on your own. There really is a rhyme and reason to what appears to be a synchronistic event. On the mystic's path, our only role is to stay open to possibilities for personal revelations.

Turkey – City of Ephesus

My tour continued with a stop in Turkey to visit the ancient city of Ephesus. I was also excited to visit another one of the cities that was mentioned in the Bible. This city was built amid a mountain and could not be easily seen from the Mediterranean Sea unless approached from a certain angle. We entered the ancient city from the top and walked towards the sea. We first passed the chambers where the politicians gathered. Next we passed the temples where Gods were honored. As we continued down the marble slabs which were used for streets we turned the corner at a giant two story building with massive columns and a big plaza in front. I was told that was the Library.

As we passed the Library, we were shown a bathhouse and then the memories started. I began to ask the guide questions seeking confirmation to things I felt I knew. For instance, I mentioned the way the city was light at night and the guide confirmed. I had this sense that the city was really crowded during its height in popularity. The guide stated that at the time of Paul's arrival, the city had a population of 250,000 people. As we came upon the final tourist spot, my jaw dropped as I looked up at the stadium. This stadium holds 25,000 people and was in wonderful condition as if it were recently built. As we sat in the stadium, we were told that Paul had filled this place when he delivered the teachings of Jesus. Something about Ephesus also felt familiar to me. I wondered what my connection here was.

When I got home, I simply forgot about the mystical experiences in Greece until my younger sister wanted me to join her and her girlfriends going to Sedona in the summer of 2006. I agreed to go because I loved Sedona and the Grand Canyon. I also I knew I could see Wanda, my past life regression counselor because I really wanted to know about the Corinth and Ephesus connection. Over a few days, I had a great time as always in Sedona which is such a magical place. Now it was time to drop me off for my past life regression session.

As we started the session, I agreed to have it taped so I could replay it as much as I needed to. I could not believe what I was hearing. In short, the reason I knew Corinth and Ephesus was because I was traveling with the Apostle Paul helping to spread the word of Christianity during the 1st Century A.D. Paul would often leave me in these cities as his surrogate until he returned. I am on the tape talking about how lonely I felt being in Corinth and how I did not want to stay by myself in Ephesus. Paul responds that it would be okay because there were rich men who secretly supported the messages of Jesus and they would care for me. Now I am really amazed and a little confused. It seems I was reincarnated before being a monk with St. Francis. I was a protégé of the Apostle Paul's as well. So it is true, we do have multiple lives.

From my Bible study, I knew about the spread of Christianity to Corinth and Ephesus. I also felt a close connection to Jesus from my Bible study. For some reason, I felt comfortable calling Jesus by his Aramaic name Jeshua (Yeshua) or Jesh for short. However, the regression session revealed something I was not prepared to hear. On the recording, I am having an entire conversation with Jesus as one of his female disciples! There were many things we talked about, but I remember him saying that we must first "get out of here" so we can talk freely. Get out of here meant to leave the alley ways of the city of Jerusalem. Well, I had never been to Jerusalem in this life, so I did not give that part of the recording too much credence until I went to Israel.

Robin L. Johnson

Israel - City of Jerusalem

The country of Israel is the ultimate place to experience a heightened sense of spirituality if you are Jewish, Christian or Muslim. As a Christian, many of the sacred places talked about in the Bible are in Israel. For my 50 birthday in June 2008, I had the opportunity to visit Jerusalem, Jericho, Dead Sea, Sea of Galilee, River Jordan, Nazareth and Bethlehem on the West Bank. One of the first stops in Jerusalem was to visit the "old city" which is the site of the original walled city of Jerusalem.

As we entered the city to retrace the "stations of the cross" where Jesus walked during his crucifixion, I was stunned to see these little alley ways with many shops and even more people. I felt relaxed in this environment which was unusual for me considering I hated crowds especially in small places. The hustle and bustle of this place felt strangely familiar as we walked the old city seeing the sites for 4 hours.

It was when we reached the Church of the Holy Sepulcher that I felt a little anxiety. This is the place where Jesus is reported to have been hung on the cross. Now a church was built on the site with the cross inside. As we entered the church and came up the steps to see the cross, I felt that familiar tension and chills that run through my body that comes when something mystical is about to happen. When I stood in front of the cross, I felt the same kind of feeling as when I stood in front of the remains of St. Francis. There was an overwhelming sense of sadness. But, I also felt the need to cry hysterically which I was having trouble suppressing as my stomach was in knots. Little tears escaped from my eyes before I heard our guide say, "okay, this way". We finished our walking tour seeing the Dome of the Rock, Western Wall and from a distance the Garden of Gethsemane.

The next day, we left the city of Jerusalem on the road to Jericho which leads past Qumran where the Dead Sea Scrolls were found. All I can think of is how blessed I am to be able to actually see the holy land to have a frame of reference for one of the holiest books on earth, the Bible. When we finally arrived at the Dead Sea, I was so excited to be able to put on the mud and float in the water. The Dead Sea is below sea level and has a salt content that does not allow for human life. Seeing the Dead Sea from land, it looks like any other large body of water with its very blue-green tint surrounded by sand. However, as soon as you enter the Dead Sea you lose your footing because the salt content forces you to immediately float. Rather you can swim or not, no matter how much you weigh, you are guaranteed to float.

So being the swimmer that I was, I absolutely loved it. I stretched out on my back with my legs crossed and my arms under my head falling into a light weight nap. At that time, I remember asking Jesus to assist me in my life with all that was meant for me to do. All of a sudden, I felt pressure on my forehead like someone was pressing me down. I was taken by such surprise that I immediately opened my eyes and started flailing in the water. Of course, no one was there. I got out of the water shortly after that experience, with a wry smile on my face, thinking do the mystical wonders ever cease? My visits to the other holy places in Israel were fairly uneventful with the exception of the sense of belonging when visiting Capernaum, home of Peter along the Sea of Galilee. All too soon the time had come to say good-bye to Israel for since it was my 50th birthday, next stop was Egypt.

Chapter 9

Land of the Pharaohs

With my head spinning from such a spiritual experience in Israel, I was truly open to the mystery of being in Egypt. As we flew on El Al from Tel Aviv to Cairo, my mind drifted back to a conversation I had two years ago with someone over dreams vs. fantasies. I told this person that I would go to Egypt for my 50th birthday. She asked a series of logical questions like: Do you have the funding? Have you made reservations? Can you get the time off of work? Of course the answer to all of the questions at that time was "no". So she proceeded to say that going to Egypt is just a "fantasy" in my mind because I had no plan to make it happen.

I laughed then said "it is a vision that will come true". What is the difference between a "fantasy" and a "vision" she asked? I told her a vision is something you have faith and confidence will occur, but you just don't know the details of the "how". As I dozed off, heading towards Egypt, I guess I was right.

Touring Egypt

It is funny that I would pick Egypt to celebrate my 50th birthday especially since I never felt any real connection to Egypt. I did "not" read many books about the ancient culture in the "Land of the Pharaohs" but was going because like most people I was fascinated by the architectural precision of the pyramids. It has been almost 5,000 years since the first pyramid at Saqqara was built and no scientist to date has been able to conclusively determine how the pyramids were constructed. Imagine my delight to find that the Mena House Hotel where we were staying was located on the Giza plateau with an unobstructed view of the pyramids from the dining room.

The trip started out like any other with my family, we first rest then we shop and or sightsee. We quickly befriended a local store owner who gave us an insider's view of Egypt. We were taken by private car to the jewelry store where we could buy cartouches which are carved ancient hieroglyphics symbols of your name on a small gold medallion. Initially designed and worn only by the Pharaohs and their royal family members because they were thought to provide protection from danger. As evening approached, my family and I had the adventure of a lifetime as we each climbed upon a camel for a ride in the desert at sunset. As I went to sleep that night, I felt like I could go home now because I had gotten everything I came to Egypt to experience. Little did I know the fun was just beginning!

Home Again

The next day we met our official tour guide named Sammy whose job it was to spend the next 12 days showing us the temples and other sacred sites of ancient Egypt. He briefed us for about an hour about the details of our itinerary.

Towards the end of the conversation he turned to me and asked, "Do you believe in reincarnation? I laughed and said "yes" given what I had experienced to date. He replied, "Good because I believe you are from here". I remember thinking, "Yeah… right". He caught my attention when he began talking to me about my spiritual nature which he had no way of knowing. He then asked if I would be willing to follow his lead to further explore my connection to Egypt. I then asked what was it he wanted me to do? He said that over the next 12 days as we move around Egypt, he would point out the sacred parts of each temple and that I should break off from the group and go there to pray. I liked the idea and said I would be more than willing to do that.

The following day after entering one the pyramids on the Giza plateau, my guide Sammy pointed out the remains of a temple nearby and said for me to start my prayers over there. He also said to ignore the guards who will surely want to make you move since it is a restricted area. After viewing the pyramid, I walked to the Temple area finding a nice spot staring at an unobstructed view of the pyramids. I then folded my hands in prayer and retreated into the silence. As I sat there in prayer I could see the guard coming from the corner of my eye. I continued to pray for openness to absorb everything this new adventure was showing me and to thank God for this opportunity to visit Egypt. As the guard caught my eye, he smiled, and then walked a few feet away and stood guard while I was finishing my prayers. On the way back to the bus, I felt strangely calm and had a brief conversation with my guide about what I had done. He said that was only the beginning. For the next few days we saw the sights and did shopping in and around Cairo before heading over to Alexandria on the Mediterranean Sea.

It was hard to imagine but the desire to see the ancient civilizations of the Western World had been completed for I had now experienced the empires of Rome, Greece, Turkey and now Egypt. Now it was time to leave the city of Cairo for our flight south to Luxor to begin our cruise down the Nile River. Although we arrived late, we got up very early to visit the Valley of Kings and Valley of Queens on the West Bank of the Nile. This is the site where the tomb of King Tut was discovered.

Mystery at Luxor and Karnak

The mystical experiences really started for me the day when we visited the Temple at Luxor. As we entered the temple, I had a strange but familiar feeling. Before I could catch myself, I instinctively asked my mother, "Where is the rest of it?" She said "What are you talking about"? I replied, "The rest of the temple, it is a lot bigger than what we are seeing here. There were many ways to enter the temple". As we began our tour, the guide reminded me that I was to be shown sacred places in each temple. Inside the Temple of Luxor he immediately took me to one such place where legend has it that you will see many visions if you place your forehead against this particular stone which had been blackened from many believers engaging in this practice. So, as I placed my head against the stone, my guide stood back and watched. I felt a little silly doing this wondering what I was supposed to be feeling when out of nowhere came this sobbing from within me as I saw flashes of my life in Egypt. When I turned to see if my guide was still there, he nodded and smiled as he walked away. I stayed only a few more moments in that spot before finishing my tour of the temple. The overwhelming size of the statues and columns cannot be adequately described and pictures do not do the Temple justice. To see statues that are tall as an 8 story buildings is mind blowing.

That night when I went to sleep I had a dream. I saw myself dressed in the white robe of a priestess walking through the torch lit temple in the evening. I remember coming from a very restricted area of the temple that was reserved for members of the royal family. Somehow instinctively, I knew I was related to the Pharaoh. The next day, I relayed my dream to my guide who confirmed that the inner sanctum of the temple was not open to the public but only to priests and royal family members. I also discovered that one of the daughters of the Pharaoh Ramses II and wife Nefertari was a priestess...interesting?

As we traveled to Karnak, we entered another temple. Our guide then said that this temple and the temple we saw yesterday at Luxor were one temple with as many as 12 gates to enter the temple. In the ancient times, the two temples together were called the "Temple at Thebes". So I was right, there were many ways to enter the temple. It was explained that the two temples were connected by a two mile long walkway originally lined with rams and sphinx statues.

During our visit to the Temple of Karnak, we had the rare opportunity to see the 10 foot high black stone statue of the Goddess Sekhmet. I say rare because this section of the temple had been closed to visitors because of the usual spontaneous healings and visions that were reported by many visitors. My guide gained access and allowed me to be the first one to enter the dark room.

Once I entered, I stood transfixed staring at the black basalt statue with the head of a lioness and the body of a woman. The Goddess Sekhmet is associated with healing energy which comes first by annihilating self-sabotaging energies, behaviors and beliefs that separate individuals from their conscious connection to the light as symbolized by the God Ra. After everyone left the small room finished with taking photos, I walked up closer to get a better look at the statue. For no reason I can identify, I felt tears start to fall as I stared at the statute. The tears continued to fall until a guard took my hand and put it on the statue's arm even though it was forbidden to touch the statue. At that point, the tears stopped and my body became instantly calm. It was time to now leave, but not before I ran back to get a quick hug of the statute. There is something about this moment that left a permanent imprint on my soul.

I really believed my mystical experiences in Egypt were now over until we made our last stop in the Temple of Karnak. We visited the wading pool used by the priests and priestesses to cleanse their bodies before entering the sacred places in the temple. The pool was filled with the waters of the Nile. Since our tour was now over and we had free time, it was all I could do to hold myself back from just jumping in the sacred water. Instead of doing that, I just wanted to stay there and meditate. Breaking my internal conversation was my sister asking, "How do we get out of here"? I remember saying in a terse voice, "Do you see that third large column, when you get there, take a left?" Never mind how I knew that was true even though we had not come that way. By this time, my family is kind of use to me with my knowledge of places I have never visited before. They seemed hesitant to go without me, so I bid the wading pool goodbye and guiding them according to the directions I had just given. We made it back to the entrance in record time.

Power Unknown

Before we boarded our boat to continue our cruise down the Nile River to the Aswan Dam, we stopped at an essential oil factory in Luxor. The guide told me that he was going to have the presenter speak to me briefly about my connection to the Goddess Sekhmet. When the presenter came over and began talking to me, he stopped in mid-sentence and said, "Oh my god, you are back" as he kissed my hand. He then asked if he could give me a hug. I thought it was cute, so I said "sure".

When the two second hug was over, this guy went instantly flush with fever and was sweating like he had a temperature. I immediately started to apologize for I did not intend to hurt him. He laughed and said it was the energy of Sekhmet. He shared a little about this deity and knew it well because his name was the masculine form of Sekhmet. As we ended he told me that I have not even begun to bring the energy that was within me but that I should take some special essential oils which would help me begin to open up my energy centers. The essential oils that he bottled for my daily use were frankincense and myrrh.

"Oh my God", I can't handle anything else. The spiritual experiences from Israel and now Egypt have left my head spinning in a way I can't even begin to explain. As our journey came to a conclusion, I was left in shock and awe by not only the beauty of this city in the desert, but now my place having walked among its people in a past life. Where does this past life phenomenon end?

Chapter 10

Saints of Asia

I have always been fascinated with Asia in particular China (Ming Dynasty), India (Siddhartha the Buddha), and Thailand (Kingdom of Siam). I have been blessed with the opportunity to visit these countries and experience first-hand their cultural traditions. In China walking the Great Wall and visiting the Forbidden City helped me to greatly understand the Ming Dynasty (Golden Age) period of Chinese history. Also, interacting with the people of China gave me insight into their spiritual philosophy as stated by Confucius and Lao-Tzu. Unfortunately, my visit to China yielded no special mystical experience such as was experienced with the Saints in India and Thailand.

India

I have been part of the masses of people in the West who have been fascinated by the cultures of the East in particular the spiritual traditions of India. It was my study of World Religions that gave me the opportunity to study Hinduism and become acquainted with Shiva and Vishnu. I was totally turned on by my reading of the "Autobiography of a Yogi" which gave me the incentive to read one of the most sacred books in the Hindu tradition, "The Bhagivad Gita". So when I was given the opportunity to travel to Jaipur, India for the Global Peace Initiative Conference, I was totally excited.

Unfortunately, when I landed in India, I was quickly a victim of rapid manifestation of my own thought process. Usually, there is ample time allowed between your thought and the manifestation of that thought. However in India, I felt that time was drastically shortened. For instance, I had been traveling for almost 18 hours before landing in New Delhi with still another 4 hours before making connection to the city of Jaipur.

When I came through customs, I was told to go to the "correspondence lounge" upstairs. I eventually found a lounge with many people waiting even though it was 2:00 a.m. but I was never sure if this was the right place since no one confirmed it for me. I sat down next to this young Indian guy who told me he was a Christian from the southern part of India where St. Thomas had brought Christianity almost 2,000 years ago. I never thought about India being anything other than Hindu in their religious traditions. Anyhow, as we continued to chat, he asked me where I was going and I told him at which point he said he thought I might have been at the wrong terminal because the flights here were international. Immediately I panicked and asked him where did I need to go? He said to take a taxi to the other side of the terminal grounds to the domestic airlines by way of the highway, it was not far. I gathered up my bags and headed out the door at about 3:30 a.m. in a taxi. I was promptly deposited at the other side of the terminal for a fee equivalent to $30.

Once there, I waited for the domestic terminal building to open at 5:00 a.m. When it did, I entered and found that

I was in the wrong place and needed to go back to where I came from. I was told to wait while someone found me a taxi. Now I was beginning to panic again because my flight was scheduled to leave a little after 6:00 a.m. One of the airline representatives agreed to get me a ride back to the international side of the airport. After all of the negotiation in Hindi and payment in advance, I was deposited to the other side of the airport. At this point, by my calculations, this little escapade cost me $100 on a ride that I was told later should have cost $5 each way!

Now I am frantic and upset about where to go and how to get my flight in an airport that is alive and teaming with people. The line back through customs was long. I would never make my connecting flight to Jaipur. I continued to ask where the check in counter was for my flight and was told "over there" in the newly constructed terminal. When I got there, someone said, no this flight is "over there" in the old terminal. So I walked back and forth for almost 10 minutes.

Finally, I stopped right in between both terminals, closed my eyes and said with intense frustration, "God, if I don't get me some help soon, I am going home"! When I opened my eyes, the flight on the marquee of the check-in stand right in front of me said Jaipur. As I approached, this lady from Pakistan took one look at me and asked if I was heading to the conference in Jaipur. I said "yes" and she said okay "Come go with me". She had special security clearance to by-pass customs, spoke Hindi and had a driver waiting for her when we arrived in Jaipur to take us to the hotel. From that point forward, I was very careful with my thoughts, they seemed to manifest very rapidly in India.

The conference in Jaipur was wonderful as we explored many topics from wars to environment and how to bring the sacred feminine energy to these situations. A few days into the conference I was given the opportunity to go to a "darshan" which is a religious healing program with a revered Saint. In this case the darshan was with Amma also known as the "Hugging Saint". Amma is one of India's spiritual leaders who in her lifetime has been known to bring love by hugging over 25 million people worldwide. I knew of Amma through her travels to the U.S., but to have this experience in India was awesome. There were 15 women from the conference who agreed to attend this special ceremony.

During the program, there were readings in Hindi followed by chanting and music. This went on for about one hour before Amma prepared herself to receive the 10,000 people in the soccer stadium who wanted to hug her. Since we were part of the women's conference, we sat right up front. As Amma started her final ritual, my body became really agitated. The more Amma waved her hand in front of her heart in a fanning motion, the worse my body felt. I was rocking back and forth, holding my heart with tears in my eyes. The energy pulsating through me was indescribable and unbearable. One of the ladies with me said you are having trouble processing the energy from Amma, so quickly take off your shoes and rub your feet on the earth to help ground yourself. That helped some, but I was much better when Amma stopped waving her hand in front of her heart.

Now it was time for Amma to receive all of those who wanted a "healing" hug. Since we were sitting up front, we were part of the first group to get in line. As I neared Amma, I started to feel this energy creeping up again as I started to feel chills. When my turn came to hug Amma, my body was shaking like a leaf. After a quick hug, I started to pull away but Amma did not let go of me until the shaking had completely stopped. She then smiled at me as she let go. Being part of the women's conference, I was then instructed to sit on the stage behind Amma to watch the rest of the ritual. After a few hours of chatting on stage with other participants, I came to find out that the encounter I had with Amma involved the transfer of "shakti". In Hinduism, shakti is a divine force which manifests to destroy evil while restoring balance, power and creativity. As we returned once again to our hotel, I will forever take away from India what it feels like to be healed by a Saint.

Thailand

When I was in college, it was from my first reading of the book about Siddhartha becoming the Buddha by Herman Hesse that cemented my love for Eastern spirituality. Although the Buddha was born in India, his spiritual philosophy is practiced more widely in other Asian countries such as Thailand where 90% of the people are Buddhist. It was by chance that I had the opportunity to visit Thailand because I had friends who were consulting with the U.S. State Department. We talked about where to rendezvous in Asia because although they had spent time in Thailand, they were now working in Vietnam.

During one of the conversations, we talked extensively about meeting in Thailand which would allow us to see a Buddhist Nun named Mae Chee Sansanee. My friend Dany (Danielle) had learned much about Mae Chee while living in Bangkok, but never had the opportunity to see her. I said to Dany that I knew Mae Chee and if I come to Thailand we could visit her together. Dany immediately thought I misunderstood her and continued to explain the saintly status of this person. I confirmed that I knew who she was talking about and to prove it I sent her a video on the life of Mae Chee. When Dany called me back, she asked me how I could live in Philadelphia and possibly know a saint in Thailand. I smiled and said I had breakfast with her in

India during the women's conference. What I remembered about Mae Chee was her amazing gentle spirit. Through her interpreter I was invited to visit her anytime I came to Thailand. Now the rendezvous in Thailand was set.

In the morning for years, I would often pray to Buddha along with Jesus, St. Francis and St. Germaine but I was excited to bring something back from Thailand to put in Buddha's corner in my meditation room. Knowing that not many people can get the time or have the money to travel to Asia, I asked the only person I knew who might say "yes" in traveling with me…my mother. This was the only region of the world that my mother had never been to during her working career and now being retired wanted to complete her world tour.

What surprised me is that she also gave this trip to my nephew as a graduation gift from high school! This kid will be starting college with travel to five countries and three continents already under his belt. When I chatted with my nephew Marcus about the impending trip, he said that he always wanted to go to Thailand. When I was his age, I cannot remember having regular conversations about Thailand, much less wanting to visit there. My nephew had friends from Asia and knew much about the culture. What a brand new world we live in.

After a 22 hour long flight, we landed in Bangkok in the middle of the night. While I peered out the window from the taxi to the drive downtown Bangkok, I was disappointed that I could not see much in the dark except a convenience store named "7-11" which we have many of in Philadelphia. So already, I felt a touch of home. It did not take long the next day to find McDonalds and Starbucks.

As we arranged our rendezvous with our friends, we learned a lot about the Thai culture. One of the first things I noticed is that the Buddhist religion in Thailand is more than just a religion; it is a way of life. By that I mean, even in Bangkok a city of 9 million people, there are what they call "spirit houses" all over downtown. These are small monuments to people who have lived on that spot which now another hotel or office building occupies. These little monuments are created as a way to honor the "Buddha Spirit" of those who use to reside there. As people walk up and down the streets of downtown Bangkok, they would routinely stop to pay respect to the spirit houses by placing incenses or flowers on the monument.

What was most memorable about Thailand is the attitude in which the people proceed with daily life. With an overwhelming majority of the people practicing Buddhism, I felt a sincere calm whenever I moved through the downtown area. People were very calm and orderly as hundreds of people lined up on the train platforms during rush hour. They entered the trains with no pushing or shoving. The manner of those in service was unbelievably cooperative, going out of their way to grant your requests. To me they put the meaning back in the term "customer service".

After being in Bangkok for a couple of days, the plans were set for us to see the Buddhist Nun Mae Chee Sansanee. We ordered a taxi from the hotel and rode about one hour from the downtown area to the Buddhist Center of Mae Chee. Upon arrival, we were met by Joy, her assistant and English interpreter who showed us around the center. Inside the walls of the center was like being in a tropical forest with lots of trees and birds singing completely blocking out the idea that you are still in a big city.

With my heart wide open, our little delegation headed to hear the morning lecture of Mae Chee Sansanee. As we sat down and participated in the opening ritual, Joy said she would be right back as she went to inform Mae Chee of our official arrival. Soon, we found ourselves sitting very near the stage. After a brief introduction, I was given the microphone to bring greetings from my delegation to her audience of 200 people and to thank Mae Chee for the invitation. We sat for the next couple of hours to listen to Mae Chee speak on the tenants of Buddhism and the need to release ourselves from unnecessary confrontation with each other. At the end of her speech, Mae Chee personally greeted each of us and we could feel once again the calming and healing energy of one of the Saints of Asia.

This visit to Mae Chee is also remembered for a mystical experience I had just before her speech. I was taking pictures of this tropical paradise when I was asked to rejoin the group as they entered this small building. Everyone was asked to leave their shoes outside as they entered. Once inside, it was extremely well lit as the room was surrounded with floor to ceiling windows and siting in the middle of the room was a gold and glass pyramid structure with small candles around the base. As I stepped into the room, the hairs on my body stood up and I began the familiar shaking and chills that accompanies being in the presence of spiritual greatness. Without knowing why I was feeling a deep sadness like I wanted to cry as I put my purse and camera down in the corner of the room.

As we gathered around the gold and glass pyramid structure, Joy spoke in perfect English to our small delegation as she explained the basic Buddhist beliefs of the Four Noble Truths. She went on to say that Buddha was the founder of their religious belief system and that the gold and glass pyramid tip houses one of the original bones of the Buddha. Oh my God, that explains the feeling I was having as I entered the small building. As we did the customary ritual around the gold and glass pyramid, I had never felt closer to the Buddha than I did at that moment. When we exited the building, it was customary to water the nearby Bodhi tree which is similar to the one Buddha sat under when he reached enlightenment. As I talked with my friend Dany she was so excited to share her experience of the room. It turns out that she felt chills upon entering and so did my nephew. All three of us were sharing a mystical experience.

No visit to Thailand is complete without a visit to the Wats (Temples) which line the river that cuts through Bangkok. Given our time constraints, I chose to visit Wat Pho where we were able to see the enlightened Buddha which is a golden statue of Buddha lying on his side with his head resting on his hands. What makes this statue so magnificent is that the Buddha on his side measures eight stories in length. After seeing the main attraction, we continued our walk through the Wat. It is a large place with many separate buildings inside each is a giant gold Buddha. What makes each building unique is that each Buddha has different poses or mudras (hand positions which convey different messages).

I was particularly attracted to one of the small buildings where there were very few people. I went up the steps, into the small sanctuary and sat down right underneath the solid gold Buddha. In the quiet, just looking up at the meditative eyes of the Buddha, I started to cry softly. I thanked the Buddha for my ability to have such an extraordinary adventure in Thailand. As I continued to express my gratitude and got ready to leave, telepathically I could hear Buddha say it is time to "walk gently upon the earth."

Chapter 11

Incan Messages

"Come go with my group to Peru, I will take really good care of you, I promise" said Gregg Braden to me as he was preparing for his lecture at the Celebrate Your Life Conference in Phoenix, AZ. As I sat and listened to his presentation, I was amazed with how this Modern Master had successfully combined science and spirituality. I decided that when I go to Peru, it would definitely be on a tour led by Gregg Braden.

Decision to Go To Peru

Over next few months as 2008 came to a close, like most people, I was enmeshed in work so I did not give much thought to officially signing up for the Peru trip scheduled for the summer of 2009. Over the Christmas holidays, I had some customary visiting to do including a visit to my aunt's house for the annual Christmas Brunch. If you did not get there early, you would miss out on the great food. This particular Christmas, I was moving slowly and considered not going to the brunch at all, but something in me say go even if you are late. So I got up, got dressed and went the four blocks to my aunt's house.

As I was greeting some of the 50 relatives that were still gathered, I ran into one of my cousins that I had not seen in a few years. My cousin Tim introduced me to his new wife Juana. We talked briefly about his work as a software consultant which allowed him to live in Peru. I told him I was thinking about going to Peru for a tour to Machu Picchu and he said "if you decide to go, make plans to stay an extra week so you can come and visit with us in Lima". Oh no, I can't believe this, guess this is my sign to go on tour with Gregg Braden. How fabulous would it be to visit with my cousins and have them show me around Peru's capital city then head up to Machu Picchu? The decision had been made; the trip to Peru was officially on.

Lima, No Place Like Home

In August of 2009, as I boarded the LAN Airlines flight to Lima, Peru I called my cousin to tell him that the flight was on time so he could meet me at the airport. The flight was totally uneventful. I remember counting my blessings as I recounted my world travels which have taken me to almost 40 countries over 5 continents. Another big adventure I thought, what would a visit to the home of the Incas have in store for me? As my cousin met me and took me to their home in the Miraflores section of Lima. Something about being in Lima with the style of architecture reminded me of being somewhere in California. My cousin lived just a 5 minute walk from the Pacific Ocean and around the corner from the JW Marriott Hotel and not far from the all too familiar KFC and Starbucks. I tell you, the world is truly a "global village". After spending almost a week having the best time with my cousins, it was time to say goodbye to Lima to head for the Andes Mountains.

Mystery of 2012 Clarified

As the airplane crossed the Andes Mountains, I remember leaning into the window to capture with my camera the snow-capped peaks which seemed endless, such a stunning site. I was told later that the Andes Mountain range has more than 500 mountains over 15,000 feet which is why so many of them were snow covered. When we landed in Cusco at an altitude of 11,400 ft., we were greeted by our tour leader and New York Times best-selling author Gregg Braden who is well known for blending science and spirituality. We loaded tour buses which would take us down to 10,000 ft. to Urubamba, the Sacred Valley of the Incas.

We spent the first few days in lectures with Gregg Braden where he discussed the ancient civilization of the Incas as well as concepts from his most recent book "Fractal Time". He covered such riveting topics as: advances in science and engineering of the Incan civilization; global coherence which scientifically measures human emotional magnetic frequencies; changes in the global weather patterns; cycles of time for World Ages; and the impact of the galactic alignment.

Gregg brought clarity to the mystery surrounding 2012. He told us that on December 21, 2012 two events will be happening simultaneously which rarely ever happens. The first event is our Milky Way Galaxy will cross the "galactic equator" which happens once every 26,000 years. The second event will be the ending of a 5,125 year New World Age which some believe will usher in the "Age of Aquarius" bringing oneness to our global community. To me these topics were simply fascinating.

Beauty of Machu Picchu

Like many of the mystic travelers from all over the world who were drawn to this trip, the ultimate treat for me was being able to see Machu Picchu. I had seen pictures of a city surrounded by many majestic mountains and now it was time to see it for real. We had a beautiful day as we arrived for our first look at Machu Picchu. It was indeed as beautiful as the pictures. We toured the entire city capturing breathtaking views of mountains with every turn.

The next morning we boarded buses early to take us back up to Machu Picchu for a sunrise meditation service. It was quite an amazing site to see the clouds hanging over parts of the city of Machu Picchu. As a group, we were led to a spot overlooking the mountains as we assembled for a meditation. As I looked at each one of the Mystic Travelers in our group, something began to happen in my heart. I felt so connected to all 55 people no matter which of the 13 countries they came from. As Gregg Braden led the meditation, I cannot say I heard a word he said because tears were falling from my eyes and my nose was running as my heart was being opened so wide. Approximately 15 minutes later, after I had gone through an entire pack of tissues, the meditation was over and we were given free time to do whatever we wanted in Machu Picchu until our train left at mid-afternoon.

Honoring Pachamama

As the group dispersed, I sought directions on how to get to the highest point in Machu Picchu for some private meditation time. As I started to walk in the direction I was given, I was so overcome with emotion that I sat down on one of the farming terraces allowing the rest of the pent up emotion to come out. What I found myself doing was feeling connected to not only our group, but feeling connected to everyone everywhere I had traveled in the world. In that instant, I was saddened by how we treat each other and how we treat the earth which brought on more tears. I remember sitting still looking out over the mountains and just crying for almost 2 hours with an inability to stop the tears from falling.

When I finally felt calm, I walked up to the location I was originally looking for where the entire city of Machu Picchu lay below me. I sat down in the sunshine and began to clear my chakra energy channels with a special crystal I had gotten from someone in our group.

After I finished clearing, I remember thinking that I wish I could find a quieter place to meditate since this current spot was noisy because it lay just below the Inca Trail. In that instant, I sat up and caught the eye of what appeared to be an employee approaching in a yellow polo shirt with the logo of Machu Picchu. He said "hello" and then followed with, "if you want a quiet place to meditate, you must first pay homage to Pachamama (Mother Earth)". I was stunned that he knew what I desired, so I asked him, "How did you know what I needed?" and he replied, "You told me with your mind" as in mental telepathy.

Okay, here we go, up for another mystical experience just when I thought I was done. So where do we have to go to pay homage to Pachamama? He pointed towards a big boulder along the Incan Trail to a sacred shrine which was just about a 10 minute walk. I gathered my things and off we went.

When we entered the site, I felt anxious and nervous but with a touch of his hand, I my body felt instantly calm. My guide performed a quick shaman ceremony on me gathering special herbs and rocks from the nearby forest. At the end of the ceremony, he led me to the big boulder and asked me to put my forehead against the rock and spread my arms like I was hugging the rock.

In the Incan culture, the shaman believes that Pachamama (Mother Earth) is a living entity and so the rocks can speak telepathically to the spiritually attuned individual. I was not aware of this phenomenon until I found myself having a telepathic conversation with Pachamama. I cannot recall the entire thing, I just remember starting with a sincere apology to Pachamama for the careless way we as humans have been treating Mother Earth and I vowed to do better in my own life so as not to dishonor her. The response was a big "thank you." I could hear a plea from Pachamama to help the people of the world change their thought system which would change their attitudes making it impossible for them to cause further damage to earth by over utilizing resources and causing pollution. It was also communicated that when we are aligned with the Spirit of God within us, we will not cause harm to any living thing. I thanked Pachamama for sharing.

On the way down the Incan Trail towards Machu Picchu, I asked my guide if he was a shaman and he laughed and said, though mystical powers may come through me, I will never make claim to being a shaman. He then showed me where to sit and meditate in peace. What makes this meditation experience so remarkable is that during this time there were more than 2,000 people walking around in Machu Picchu. Sure enough where he had taken me I was not disturbed by a single person for almost two hours as I communed with the beautiful snow-capped Andes Mountains all around me. When it was time for me to go, I gave thought to the idea of leaving when my guide magically appeared. As we chatted for a moment, I said I wanted to give him a small donation for his services so I took off my watch and gave it to him. He was very excited to receive such a gift. It was really a man's watch that I brought just for the trip so I would have an alarm. In some ways giving it to him symbolically released me from time.

This was one of the most amazing days I would ever experience, but the extended effect of Machu Picchu was yet to be discovered. As I was sharing with other members of my tour group about my experience, someone asked me to read something. It was only when I was half-way done that I realized I was reading without my glasses. I then thought back to the many small ailments I had when we started this trip. I had a prescription for medication for a root canal that the dentist said I needed when I got back. However, the pain in my tooth was no longer there. I had a knee brace because of swelling in one knee which also went away. The arches in my feet were beginning to collapse causing some pain but they no longer bothered me. My body felt great and my eyes were never clearer. The good news is that most of these adjustments lasted for months after the trip. The only thing that changed as I returned to the polluted urban center where I reside was that I could begin to feel some cloudiness over my eyes. However, I can still read some small print without my glasses. That was worth the visit to Peru by itself, but that was not the end of my mystical experiences there.

Trauma at Kenko

I was really in a good mood leaving Machu Picchu for a tour of the Temples of Kenko and Sachsayhuaman near the city of Cusco. As the tour bus approached the site for the Temple of Kenko, I immediately felt anxious as I stepped off of the bus. As I started walking with the group towards the Temple of Kenko, which just looked like a giant boulder, I felt this anxious feeling turn to sheer dread. This was really weird since I had never heard of this site before so I could not imagine why I was reacting like this. So I quickly chatted with one of my group members Adele and asked her if I could follow her through this site. As we passed between these two big boulders, one had an opening where you could see inside the dimly light room where Incan rituals were performed. As we filed between the boulders in single file, I barely looked into the room as I hurried past. I felt a sense of relief now that it is done.

When we met up with the group in a courtyard on the other side of the boulders, I heard an announcement that we were now going to go inside of the Temple of Kenko. With that announcement, my knees went instantly weak and I struggled to find a rock to sit on before I fell down. Did you ever have a fear of something but not know why? I decided that I would get some support and called over one of the tour guides who agreed to go in the Temple of Kenko with me. I instructed him to let me have my experience, but at some point if I seemed unable to move from a spot for him to put his hands on my shoulders and that would bring me back from whatever memory I might be caught in.

As we followed the group into the cave like structure, people were laughing and talking all around me. As for me, with each step I felt nothing but doom. I stepped up slowly into the dimly light cave known as the Temple of Kenko with my knees shaking. I walked right up to the first altar which was a stone slab that was waist- high where I was told sacrifices were made to the Gods. For no reason I can fathom, I put my hands on the stone alter and closed my eyes.

Oh my God, within an instant I was caught up in what seemed like a movie clip. What I visualized was that the temple seemed dark and lit only by torches. I saw a young woman in her early 20's with long black hair and a voluptuous body walking towards where I was standing then she passed right through my current body as she climbed up on this 4 foot high stone alter to be sacrificed. She looked stoic and unemotional. I realized that the woman I was looking at was me when I felt my emotional body screaming loudly, "I don't want to do this".

In reality, I started crying and repeating out loud over and over again, "I don't want to do this… I don't want to do this". Finally, in trying to calm myself, I began talking to my "emotional body" that was stuck in ancient times convincing it that everything turned out okay. In that moment, I felt strangely reunited with that part of myself that seemed to be missing for thousands of years. Soon enough, my guide put his hands on my shoulders and I was able to break free from the vision that I was having. As I moved through the rest of the temple in shock, I had no other feelings as I looked at other altars. Several people asked me what happened as they heard me crying out. As I shared this experience, I was given confirmation that another person on tour had a similar experience of seeing herself sacrificed while others confirmed having a "feeling" that people in addition to animals were sacrificed there.

This experience is in direct contrast to what our guides shared about sacrifices. So as soon as I found a few moments on the bus to get quiet, I sought answers from my Spirit as to the meaning of "human sacrifices" in Ancient Civilizations. The answer came back that it was an honor for any human to volunteer for such an assignment because Ancient cultures believed that nothing and no-one was more valued than God. For the person who was sacrificed, it was believed that this person assisted other members of the tribe by keeping the pathway open between heaven and earth allowing each person in death to easily reunite with God.

Final Message

I was still in a daze as we left the Temple of Kenko for the short ride to the stone ruins of Sachsayhuaman. At this new site, many in the group were talking about the energy of Sachsayhuaman and how powerful it was to those that were spiritually attuned. Someone asked me if I could feel the energy, but my mind was so busy processing the last experience that I could not bring my attention to the here and now. I listened without comprehension to the tour guide describing the stones weighing tons and their precise positioning without mortar to hold them in place in such a way as one small coin could not fit in between the stones.

When she finished talking, I approached the stones with arms outstretched in a "bear hug" position and put my forehead to the rocks trying to connect to the energy of this place. It took a minute as my body got calm enough to tune in. I don't remember all that was communicated in this mystical tradition of "speaking to the rocks", but I do remember being told that "it was my turn to lead". Oh no, after 20 years of study and preparation was this the mission I had agreed to do based on my dream of talking with St. Francis. As I snapped back to reality, I remember saying telepathically to the rocks with a lot of emotion, "I am not ready". But, the response that came back was "do not worry it will be as easy as breathing". With that, all of the "Incan Messages" had been communicated.

Sharing Mystical Experiences

During the trip to Peru, it was indeed a pleasure to meet so many people on a mystical journey from so many different countries. We had life coaches, healers, energy workers, clairvoyants, regression therapists and more. Our leader Gregg Braden nicknamed us the "Mystic Travelers".

As the trip progressed, I tried to get around to talking with most of them, but time did not permit me to visit extensively with everyone.

As time was running out and the trip was coming to an end, I remember I wanted to talk with Diane who I heard had been doing some fabulous things regarding spiritual issues at the United Nations in New York City. Since I had spent a decade dealing with international organizations, I thought it would be fascinating to talk to her about her international work. It took a minute as we often found ourselves engaged in conversations with others.

Diane and I finally found our opportunity to talk as we had hours together riding the train to Lake Titicaca located some 12,000 feet up on the high plains in the Andes Mountains. We sat down at the back of the train looking at the sunset through the big picture windows and began our conversation. It started with Diane remarking about how similar the landscape was to Mongolia. I soon realized that not only had Diane visited many of the world's spiritual places, but that she too had experienced her share of mystical experiences in many of them as well. We both laughed as we shared our individual "messages from the rocks" in Machu Picchu. I remember we talked about our respective visits to Greece, Israel, Italy, and India. We also discussed the same books we read and the same Modern Masters we heard present. All too soon we ran out of time as we approached our destination -- Lake Titicaca.

Interesting conversations never really end, they just have long pauses. The next morning I found myself up early wanting to take a short walk. Guess who else was up having the same thought? You got it, Diane. So we agreed to walk the paved road in front of the hotel. Our conversation continued like that of two old friends so delighted to be in each other's company again. We concluded after sharing experiences that we must be from the same "soul family" traveling through time and space together.

On our way back up the road towards the hotel, we saw at least six llamas and alpacas heading toward us as the hotel staff were forcing the animals to leave the grounds. I remember saying to Diane, I wonder where they are going? I learned later that groups of llamas and alpacas just roam freely as they are considered sacred animals in Peru. It is often said that you will know a person's spirit by the reaction of animals who can feel the energy of your intention. I was curious as to what these animals would do when they encountered us.

I remember looking at a brown alpaca and wishing it would come closer. Well, wouldn't you know it walked right up to Diane and me! When I reached out to touch it, it pulled back slightly. I continued to extend my hand slowly and gently and it soon let me pet it. As I stood staring directly into its eyes, I could not help but feel a similar connection to the camel that I rode in Egypt. Can you image any wild animal letting humans close enough to pet it? I guess we can add that one to our growing list of mystical experiences.

Part III

Delicious

Chapter 12

Closer to Home

To me "delicious" moments are similar to "aha" moments; it is when you reach a new understanding of some belief or situation. It does not mean life no longer has challenges, but that the challenges are dealt with from a completely new perspective making evolution a much easier process. Now that is "delicious"...

Let me take you through an experience I had in New York City so you can easily see what I am talking about. I was really excited about an opportunity to see Thich Nhat Hanh, Buddhist Monk from Vietnam, especially since I had read his book entitled "Peace Is Every Step". This encounter with Thich Nhat Hanh was both mystical and delicious.

Buddhist Monk Shares

As I sat in the audience with my friend Kristina participating in the opening chants, I realized how we really live in a global village. The audience was a mixture of every ethnic group you could think of coming to hear a Buddhist Monk from Vietnam. Amazing...As a human family, we are beginning to embrace our commonality as we let go of the concepts that reinforce our differences. As the program went on, I was feeling much gratitude in my heart for my life and the great adventures I have been blessed to experience especially in the last two years.

Now approaching the stage was Thich Nhat Hanh and the audience stood while the cameras went crazy. As Thich Nhat Hanh took a seat, the chanting intensified with his followers singing in harmony with each other and a singing bowl being struck accordingly. This process went on for approximately 15 minutes before Thich Nhat Hanh appeared to be entering a meditative state. As part of that process, he continued to move his open hand to his heart then pull away from his heart with just two fingers and release the two fingers into the air. He repeated this motion over and over again.

To my surprise, this motion of Thich Nhat Hanh moving his hand to his heart began to remind me of my experience with Amma in India. I began to wiggle in my chair as I felt the energy moving through me. It seems as if I have gotten used to tuning in to the smallest of mystical experiences. My heart felt like it was exploding every time Thich Nhat Hanh pulled his hand away from his heart. I just kept thinking I wish he would hurry up and stop, I cannot handle much more. I am sure the practice had something to do with binding our energies together as one group because as he continued with this motion, the audience got quieter and quieter. Finally he had stopped and his lecture began. Yes, finally a chance to relax and exhale.

Thich Nhat Hanh spoke much about the way we live our lives especially in the West in such a way as to stay distracted from being one with our inner selves. He talked also about being mindful of everything you do as you move through life. He spent a few extra minutes talking about the

Lotus flower which grows in India. What makes this flower so interesting he explained is that in order for it to reach its full beauty, it must grow in the mud. Thich Nhat Hanh then drew parallels between the flower and the way we live our lives spending some time in the mud.

Out of Control

Overall, I got what I came for in terms of the philosophy of the message but I actually was awakened to the experience of the message by the lady sitting next to me. As mentioned earlier, the program started with chanting and then a meditation. This nicely dressed young lady seeming to be in her 20's came rushing in late with her friend and sat down next to me putting her bag almost on my feet. She continued talking to her friend during the meditation but soon enough they got quiet.

When Thich Nhat Hanh came out, many people were taking pictures including me on my cell phone, but in order to avoid the heads of the people in front of me, I leaned towards this lady in snapping a few of the pictures. She immediately said in a terse voice, "would you stop that, I am trying to concentrate". So I quietly put my camera away.

No sooner had I done what she requested then she began talking to her friend. I let it go on for a few minutes before interrupting their conversation with the comment, "Can you please stop talking"? What was interesting is that immediately, I did not feel this was the proper way to handle this situation, for what I was really angry over was being interrupted for taking pictures like everyone else. What was interesting is that I felt badly for trying to control her behavior the same way she had tried to controlled mine. I decided not respond to anything else she did for the rest of the night but to just watch her behavior instead.

As the speech went on, I was able to notice how this lady tried to control everything around her. When the person behind her was digging in her bag making noise, the lady next to me turned around and looked at the other woman with a scowl on her face. When the people got up in front of us and headed for the exit only to return a short time later, the lady next to me made a face in her agitation as she whispered something to her girlfriend. As the people on the other side of her got up to exit the auditorium, she then huffed in anger.

What was beginning to be funny to me was that this lady sitting next to me could not see herself. At one point, she did everything she was angry at everyone else for doing. It started with her digging in her bag making noise trying to find mints. Later on, she too got up and left the auditorium in the middle of the speech only to return. Shortly after that her friend got up, then left, and returned as well. The more I watched the more I became fascinated with how we cannot see ourselves and our own behavior. Being able to observe her behavior from a place that was not full of irritation was truly delicious! I continued to watch her nod as the speaker talked about being more mindful of our actions. "You have got to be kidding me!" I thought. They arrived late had lots of anxious energy with them, then 10 minutes before the speaker finished his presentation, they gathered up their belongings and permanently left.

Living on Fantasy Island

Approximately 15 minutes more had passed before my friend Kristina and I left the theater. We immediately began talking about the lady next to me. Kristina reacted the same way I did initially by criticizing the lady for being disruptive while telling me to stop taking pictures. Then Kristina asked me, why didn't I get more upset? I laughed as I said that I actually "thank" the lady because of what she showed me about myself. She was the best example of a behavior based on "fantasy". Now what does that mean?

Sometimes you can know things intellectually, but then something happens and that experience crystallizes the reality of a concept. What I realized was that like this lady, I spent my entire life trying to control the behavior of everyone and everything around me. The problem was never me, it was always them. If they would only stop talking, if they would only sit down, if they would only do the right thing, then I would be able to enjoy myself. The reason this behavior is based in fantasy is because "the problem is within". The lady thought that by stopping me from taking pictures that would somehow bring her peace. But no sooner did I acquiesce to her demand then she started making demands of others around her to stop their activities.

Trying to control the behavior of others is endless and pointless. Do you honestly believe there is anything someone else can temporarily stop doing which will cause you to experience permanent peace? I spent my life responding to requests and demands as well as issuing requests and demands thinking that controlling the outside world would bring me peace. Trying to control what is outside of me does not change what is inside of me. I have been living on "Fantasy Island".

This night, I also realized like I never have before that someone cannot change themselves by requiring me to be different. Think about that for a moment. The upsets we think are outside of ourselves causing us to behave as we do are really upsets within us that are being triggered by external events. So as I no longer felt the need to respond to the behavior of the lady next to me, it became easier for me to let go of the fantasy I was carrying about the peace that comes with controlling the behavior of others. I wonder if

Robin L. Johnson

she will ever come to understand that concept. As Thich
Nhat Hanh said during his lecture, it is in being mindful
that we experience the peace within. What a lesson to get
and to think it came so much closer to home.

Chapter 13

All is Forgiven

It is amazing with the passing of time how unimportant most conflicts seem to be as we try to understand what made us so upset in the first place. Although I was grateful for the lesson learned in New York, I was on course to learn an even bigger lesson closer to home which is "in death, all is forgiven".

Life Can Change In An Instant

As I took one last look at myself in the mirror of my hotel room, I smiled as I blew myself a kiss for looking so "jazzy" as I headed out to the Parliament of World Religions Conference at the Melbourne Convention Center. Although it was early December, it was the perfect summer day in Australia as I glanced out the hotel window. I was feeling extremely blessed to have spent one week visiting Melbourne and Sydney. As far as I was concerned, this "officially" completed my world tour having visited all major continents. I had the best time in Australia with my cousins Pam and Tracey who flew in for the conference as well and my local life coaching friends Martyn and Heather who truly showed me what "Aussie hospitality" was all about.

As I picked up my purse, I felt a sharp pain go up my spine and across the top of my shoulders. I stood ramrod straight for a few moments as I winced in pain. As soon as the pain subsided, I remember thinking I will find out soon enough what the problem is at "home". You see I know I am "clairsentient" which means I have a sixth sense which allows me to feel the intense emotions of my family and close friends no matter where I am in the world.

At the end of my day while I was packing, I decided to check the messages on my cell phone. Good thing I keep an international plan which allows people to dial my local telephone number and reach me anywhere in the world. God bless the minds that created this system. Anyway, I had several voicemail messages and a couple of text messages which informed me that my father had been hospitalized. This came as a shock to me because I did not know he was sick. Oh, how life can change in an instant. I felt relieved to understand the explanation for the earlier tension in my back and neck. When speaking to my family I jokingly said tell my dad, "He better not die on me before I get home and it will take me two days to get there!" No joke, Australia is a long way from the East Coast of the U.S. My travel itinerary had me in motion for the next 36 hours flying non-stop to Hong Kong then after staying overnight flying non-stop to New York with a short shuttle ride down to Philadelphia.

Journey Home

On my long journey home, I thought about my father and the good memories we shared. The last time I had seen him at my house was just the month before I headed off to Australia. He drove up to my house to show me his latest car which was his usual "Cadillac". You see my father was a "cool breeze" and handsome kind of guy with his stocky build, thick mustache and nice brim always covering his wavy salt and pepper hair. When I think about my father's lifestyle I can say he was a guy who never truly mastered his appetites for the pleasures of the world, if you get my drift. Unfortunately, his passions for life's pleasures took its toll on his relationships with his two wives and seven children.

One of the reasons I was close with my father is because I took the time to work out my residual emotions of anger and frustration with him. We had really come to understand and appreciate each other as we gathered quarterly for breakfast. I always knew when it was time because I would get a call from my father saying, "Hey Precious, when are we going to breakfast?" With that thought on my mind, I dozed off to sleep on the flight from Hong Kong to New York.

Do mystical wonders ever cease? I did not know how long I was asleep before I heard a voice call my name "Robin". In somewhat of a stupor I remember answering "Yes, who is that?" because I did not recognize the female voice. "Edna" was the response. She was my father's oldest sister who died a few years ago. I then asked, "Is he dead?" The answer quickly came back "no" and with that I went back into a deep sleep until I landed in New York.

Not Much Time

Although I was tired, the first thing I wanted to do was to see my father. I did not trust myself to drive, so my older sister Pamela agreed to take me to the hospital. When I saw my father for the first time, it was like being on the set of the movie "Avatars" for my father's completely yellow eyes were glazed over in a "death stare" as he moved his head in slow motion to the sound of someone's voice. I was completely devastated by what I saw. It was at this time that I learned that his illness was undiagnosed colon cancer which had spread to his kidneys making it inoperable. I also learned that as I was flying back from Australia he was in a coma with great concern on the part of my family that he might never wake up. So seeing him like that was an improvement.

The fact that he was alive was great but the prognosis was he did not have much time with a maximum of six months to live. The truth was that from the moment I saw him in the hospital until his death was more like 30 days. My father elected to go home for hospice care and so the routine of visiting and calling him begun. Initially, he was full of life and excited to be home receiving all visitors who wanted to spend time with him. As the days turned into weeks, his health increasingly declined as paralysis set in.

With his initial decline came my total "meltdown" as jet- lag set in. I was unable to get myself together to see him or call him for a week. I sat in a comatose state in my pajamas crying off and on as I listened to Michael Jackson's song, "Gone Too Soon". At times, I was crying about my father's impending death and other times I had no thoughts in my mind, just this overwhelming feeling of sadness. I eventually realized that during traumatic times in my life I never cried. So during this week I released a lifetime of unhealed emotionality. I also discovered that throughout my life it was my anger which masked my deep sadness.

During this time, I reached out to Spring, my friend and life coach who just a few short years before had a similar experience of losing her father during the Christmas holidays. In talking to her, I found her understanding, compassionate, warm, loving and supportive of my process. I found space with her to begin to articulate what I was actually feeling which helped me immensely come to terms with the idea my father was dying.

I was not prepared for the fact that everyone else in my family did not feel exactly as I did. As I was cycling through my emotions mainly feelings of sadness, I was surprised to be greeted by anger or hostility from other family members when talking about my father. My friend Debbie finally asked me, "Don't they have a right to feel as they do?" With that I had to agree. My mother also added that "grieving is a very personal process" since no two people have the same relationship with the dying person. It was during this time that I learned I needed to feel my own emotions without the need for others to validate what I was feeling.

Death will get us to see things differently. I never had a second thought about telling someone "I will talk to you tomorrow". However now when I used that phrase with my father it was greeted with "if I am alive" for he was truly living on borrowed time. It became increasingly difficult to have a conversation with him because I realized much of what I talked about was based on what I was "going to do". Very soon, I found myself beginning to live my life in a "moment to moment" fashion as taught by Thich Nhat Hanh.

Christmas Blessings

On Christmas day, I woke up and my first call was to my father to see if he was still alive and up for visitors. When the answer was yes, I made plans to drive the 30 minutes to his home even though there was still much snow around from the blizzard in Philadelphia just a few days before. Shortly after I arrived, my brother Marshall came in to help move my father to his favorite recliner for that was my father's Christmas wish.

For the next couple of hours, life seemed normal as we all sat around watching the professional basketball games. At the end of one game between the Miami Heat and the

New York Knicks, my Aunt Mattie (father's remaining sister) asked me to feed my father. I grudging did for it was a little heartbreaking for me to have to feed him with a spoon and give him liquids through a straw. There was however a funny moment when I found the spoon suspended in mid-air with food on it while I watched Dwayne Wade of the Miami Heat split two defenders at the foul line then dunk the ball over another two defenders. I remember turning to my father and saying, "oops, sorry daddy, that was a good play". He just smiled. After the game, I sat a little while longer with my father stroking his hair and holding his hand as he sat in his recliner. Our communication had been reduced to me squeezing his hand from time to time and him squeezing back.

As I drove home that day I felt really happy that I got to spend one last Christmas with my father. Between Christmas Day and New Year's Eve, I went to church three times in seven days and each time I said a special prayer for my dad. On New Year's Day of 2010, I called to wish my father a "Happy New Year" and thank him for making it through the holidays. I also reminded him that when he made his transition he could still talk to me telepathically because I would definitely answer. He just chuckled and in a slow voice said, "Thank you Baby, I love you, God bless". Little did I know these would be the last words I would ever hear from my father for he died a few days later.

In his last days, I knew his transition was near being the clairsentient person that I am I was able to feel what was going on in my father's body. I would call my aunt or his friend to confirm his symptoms. For instance, two nights before he died, I felt intense pain in my legs and lower part of my body and no matter what I did I could not get relief. The next day it was confirmed that my father had indeed experienced such acute pain during that night that he had to be given morphine in the morning. My father also had intense anxiety which as my nephew Jonathan once said, "it is hard to die with regrets." The last night before his death, I found myself unable to breathe normally for my breathing had become intensely shallow. This even scared me for a moment as I called my sister and told her to check on me in the morning to be sure I was okay. But once again, when I checked in, it was my father having that experience as the fluid was building up in his lungs. On the actual day of my father's death, I had this feeling of lightness as I walked through the park in the early afternoon sunshine. When I thought of my father I remembered smiling and repeating, "You are so gone". Sure enough, when I checked in that evening, I was told that my father did not open his eyes at all that day and officially died that night.

Farewell but Not Gone

As plans were made for the funeral, we had some of the usual family disagreements. However, by the time of the actual funeral, we came together to support each other through our grief. As I sat through the funeral reading the program, I was struck by the kind words and later the beautiful slide show tribute to my father's life. I came away from the church with the thought "in death, all is forgiven". I also wondered how we could bring that same level of forgiveness to each other in life. I am really glad I worked out all of my residual emotions with my father. Now whenever I think about him, it is with "unconditional love" and gratitude for having had him as my "daddy".

As I close this chapter, I just wanted to leave you with one last mystical experience which shows that we may say farewell to our loved ones but are they really gone? The day after the funeral activities I was in a state of disbelief that my father was really dead. As I gently stroked the cover of the funeral program I had big tears running down my face. I do not know how long I had been like this when all of a sudden I heard my father's voice just as clearly saying to me, "Baby, you have cried enough for me, I don't deserve it." I replied, "You are right, you don't deserve it, but I don't do it because you deserved it, I do it because I love you". With that I could hear him chuckle. As the telepathic conversation continued, he apologized for not believing me when I came back from my international travels wanting to share my mystical adventures. Due to his lack of interest, I stopped sharing.

My father also admitted that I was right in how I was seeing reality and because of my spiritual development we could easily have this kind of telepathic conversation so quickly piercing the veil between dimensions. He asked me to think of him as gone on one of my international adventures. He concluded with, "You must go on with your life for you have a lot to do". I then asked him, "Like what?" He responded, "We are not allowed to tell you that from here".

After this conversation which seemed so real and now feeling a little more energetic, I bundled myself up to take a walk in the park. At the end of my walk, I remember sitting on the bench looking across the baseball field staring towards the sunshine in a daze. I was thinking back on all I had been through in the last 30 days. I had heard of people talking about birds in connection to death, but now I was going to have my own experience.

No sooner did I finish my reverie when my attention was drawn to four large black crows flying slowly across the baseball field. As I tracked their path, they all came to perch on top of the same light pole. I immediately thought about my father and the other members of his family that preceded him in death such as his father, mother, older brother and oldest sister. As I stared at the four birds sitting together, I thought briefly, "I wonder where my father is?" Almost immediately after I said that, I saw a lone black crow flapping its wings quickly doing a big loop around the baseball field then speeding rapidly, towards the same light pole. Once there, it slowed then perched itself with the others. With that image in my mind, I laughed as I headed home.

Conclusion

A Mystic's Path

You have read my story that I share to support you on your mystic's path. Some of you may be struggling with owning your humanness while others may need confirmation of your mystical experiences. Either way I hope the information in this book was useful.

The mystic's path requires enlarging our worldview, integrating all of our human experiences, harmonizing our feeling nature, mastering our appetites, which then allow for clarity of mystical experiences. This is not a place you can arrive to on your own using your superior intellectual ability. This mystic's journey requires something bigger than you to direct your path. If you are like me then you will understand that there is nothing more valuable than listening to your Spirit which brings you into oneness with God. It is only from this place that transcendence of duality is possible and access to higher dimensions is available.

As the book has described, if you want to own your mystical side, you must clean out the vessel, "loosen the grip of your ego" and give God "room to operate" within you. Mystics have to embrace their willingness to look stupid, foolish, and ridiculous in following the voice of their Spirit, but will do so because the external judgment of others is nothing compared to the internal shift that brings permanent peace when aligning with God. Once this shift is complete we can create an "ego free zone" within ourselves allowing all of life to flow more freely.

Time for a New Understanding

A mystic's path is about forgiveness of self and others while you still have time to bring reconciliation. Because of early childhood trauma that comes to us all, the ego structure crystallizes in emotional situations where the individual feels powerless. This way of being and seeing the world takes over our adult personality and leads us to make decisions in spite of the consequences to others. On a mystic's path, this way of being that separates us from others must be interrupted.

To access how you separate yourself from others, you will have to find your own pockets of anger, guilt, fear and resentment in order release the grip of your ego. For it is not towards others that you harbor these feeling, but towards yourself. By looking deeply you will find that your anger is projected onto others because somewhere or somehow you did "not" do something that resulted in your feeling guilty. It is your inability to deal with your own guilt that leads to suppression of emotions resulting in projection. This cycle of guilt and anger followed by the suppression over past mistakes creates this constant "shadow boxing" with others driving up violence in our societies.

At some point, on a mystic's path, we must learn to separate people from their ego driven behavior for that is the only space which gives forgiveness room to operate. Once we learn to forgive others for their inability to control their egos due to their warped perceptions of reality resulting from the trauma of their childhood, then room will be given to us. We are so much more than our bad behaviors. The "essential essence" of who we really are is never touched by life's traumatic experiences.

We must also learn to cycle more quickly through our emotions like athletes or children. In any professional sport, it is the athlete who engages the opposition on the field with anger and intensity. However, at the end of the competition, they shake hands letting go of the emotion displayed in competition. Contrast this to the spectators who leave the game still steaming with anger and hatred over their team losing. Children also cycle through emotions very quickly. They go from being angry to sad to joyful all while playing with the same child.

As an adult, if you can get past hating a person's behavior, you will move towards a place of compassion for them as you understand how their way of seeing reality was a direct result of some emotional trauma. Make no mistake we are all "walking wounded". From childhood trauma, people who were bullied may become bullies, people who were victims may become victimizers and people who were poor may become greedy. But too often we forget the source of the behavior was often started as a protective measure because of a sense of powerlessness.

Takes Two to Tango

The difficulty today is that as adults when conflict and chaos erupt, few take responsibility for contributing to the chaos. Instead they anchor themselves in their own righteous positions claiming "she/he started it" or "all they need to do is…" followed by some directive from a person's ego. Believe it or not, "it takes two to tango" so when conflict erupts, the question should always be "what is my contribution to the chaos?"

The stronger the ego, the less one sees itself as having contributed to the conflict. We need to understand our part in conflict as well as the other person's role in order to bring a resolution that will bring lasting peace. If you do not own your bad decisions, your deluded sense of self will make you more likely to be critical and judgmental of others. For once you accept some fault or frailty within yourself you usually will not judge it in others.

Expanding Worldview

We all have such linear ways of looking at reality and the mystical experiences I shared here can attest to the need to expand our worldview. Initially, my mystical experiences fell into the category of "other" in my mind because of my linear, logical, analytical model of reality could not process it. I did "not" initially reject the mystical experiences I just could not welcome them with open arms. If you are honest with your emotionality by expressing the doubt, denial and fear that initially comes with mystical experiences then in time verification of the mystical events will overcome your doubt and deliver the revelation that is meant for you.

To continue to walk the mystic's path, we all must be willing to take risks moving outside of our comfort zones. Because of my 20 year career as a management consultant, I got use to taking risks. However it is not my profession that moves me forward, it is my belief in the possibility of being one with the Spirit of God in this dimension of physicality. This belief is what ultimately kept me moving beyond the things I was most afraid of. If you find yourself having fear like I did, then I encourage you to take small steps and ask for verification as I did. In time you will learn to trust the

Spirit of God within you while your external obstacles will begin to disappear.

I know I am not alone in wishing for a new planet where there is no more war, no famine, no crime, no violence, no pollution, no racial discrimination nor separation of any kind. It is towards this global vision of oneness that I have always been pulled. What would it take for this current generation of mystics to come together with the Modern Masters to create heaven on earth? I guess what makes me different is that I think this vision is not only possible but inevitable.

Pop Quizzes from the Universe

Once you feel you have arrived on the mystic's path, be prepared for the universe will always give you "pop quizzes" to ensure your understanding of concepts you think you know. Pop quiz is what I call those unexpected disharmonious events that come to interfere with the "flow of your life". These disruptive events don't give you time to think, so you can only react from an unconscious behavior pattern. If your new concept has taken root then during a pop quiz the new response will be exhibited.

Let me give you an example of a "pop-quiz" or in this case a larger "final exam". After my experience in New York with Thich Nhat Hanh, I believed I had reached some major milestone with regards to understanding the concept of "living on fantasy island" trying to change the behavior of others. Throughout my life, I was always concerned with things being perfect in my world, so you can image my anger if things got lost or were broken. I would look for someone to release my anger upon.

Well within a few weeks of the New York lecture, I say my "final exam" was given by the universe. Within three days, all sorts of things were broken or lost but I never lost my temper which was unusual. It started with my computer mouse failing. When that got fixed the keyboard failed then the printer failed. Shortly after that, I dropped and broke my keychain from Paris as I was heading into my office. When I exited my office a short time later on the same day, I again dropped my car keys and this time broke my keychain from Peru. That night at home I was on the telephone when the telephone battery died and the other phones would not reach an outside line. So I turned on my cell phone which showed "no service". My reaction during this time was one of disbelief, but not really anger.

Given all of the confusion, I decided to go to sleep but then in the middle of the night my Palm Pilot, a small device which held my telephone numbers suddenly illuminated then crashed. I could not turn it off as the blank screen starred back at me in the darkness. I must admit when this happened, all I could do was laugh.

The next day, I tried to play one of my spiritual DVDs but found the DVD player was broken. So I went to Sam's Club, bought a new DVD player. Guess what, you got it, the replacement DVD player did not work either. To resolve the issue, I ended up visiting Sam's Club three times in as many hours. During this encounter, I felt a hint of frustration but it never turned into full blown anger which it could have easily done given all that I had already been through in the last few days.

Well the universe ended its final exam a week later by causing a complete power outage in my house which lasted 3 hours crashing my cable converter box. Are you getting the picture yet? Over time everything got fixed but not necessarily on a schedule I could control. The point of my story is that whoever you think you are "being"; the universe will surely test you to see if that way of being is truly emotionally authentic for that is the only way to become one with God.

In closing this discussion, I want to clarify the concept around anger for those on the mystic's path. As mentioned, to be one with God requires authentic emotionality, so you cannot fake your way to oneness. One of the experiences most sought after by spiritual seekers is their ability to control their anger. To me, it is a paradox that as long as you are focused on controlling your anger, you are actually inhibiting the natural inclination of your emotions thereby potentially contributing to disproportionate displays of anger when it is finally released. On the other hand, if you have allowed for the full expression of any "residual emotionality" even anger, then no hidden emotion remains. Even though life's frustrations will still get you angry, the intensity is so slight that others perceive your anger as non-existent. Therein lays the secret to responding without anger.

10 Tips on the Mystic's Journey

As I close this chapter, now that you understand my philosophy of "why" it is important for more of us to awaken our mystical side, let's look at the "how". Below are some tips to support you on your mystic's journey:

1. **Identify the Voice of Your Spirit**

   Find time daily to be still -- no television, no radio, no telephone, and no conversation – just complete silence in order to identify the voice of your Spirit. This time could be in nature, in your home or even in your office for I have communed with God in all of these places. The point is that no progress can be made on the mystic's path without the ability to hear your Spirit without interruption to be able to trust in the intuitive guidance that you are receiving. You must begin to differentiate your ego from the voice of your Spirit. After a period of silence, allow yourself time to read spiritual literature which will help elevate your vibration and continue to move your thought system from an ego dominated one to a God centered one. Reading of New Age or New Thought books along with books on personal development or self-help are also helpful in creating harmonious relationships with those around you.

2. **Master Your Appetites**

In order to "clean out the vessel", you must bring yourself into emotional authenticity regarding your past bitter experiences. This also helps you as you continue to master your appetites for the pleasures of this world. If you do not clean out the vessel, then you continue to give the "ego room to hide". This results in bad decision-making as you continue to project your anger and frustration onto others. Find the source of your upset and news-flash, it is not in the behavior of other people! There is some emotion in you that needs to be identified and expressed. When you are feeling negative emotions like anger, fear, or sadness, see if you can identify the source of the emotion by asking yourself, "Where have I felt this way before?" Then

let yourself journal, freely expressing any
bottled up emotions.

3. **Own Your Mystical Experiences**

Review your life for your own mystical
experiences. Look for those experiences
that seem to defy reality. Concentrate on
conversations you may have in dreams
with religious figures (Jesus, St. Francis,
Mother Mary, Buddha, etc.). Think about
your pull to certain sacred sites around the
world whether or not you have been there.
Is there a certain time in religious history
that you seem drawn to? Do some research?
What were the issues of that time and what
are the parallels in today's world. It is time
to trust the mystical experiences you are
having for they serve to realign you with
the Spirit of God within. Journal about
them, find someone you trust to share them.
"Time to get on purpose" and owning your
mystical experiences is one way to help you
get there.

4. **Don't Share Your Vision With Everyone**

This tip is very important especially to those
new on the mystic's path. Traveling this
road is full of much uncertainty because
you are learning to trust the Spirit of God
within. Information may come in pieces
without the ability to see the entire picture,
so you may be guided to implement only
part of your vision. The last thing you
need is someone to question your vision
or implementation process, especially

when you do not have answers yourself. Doubt creates anxiety which immediately separates you from the voice of your Spirit. As you travel this path, find the right people to support you who support your mystical experiences, visions, concerns or insights. If you don't have anybody available, it may be helpful to connect to the communities of the various Modern Masters mentioned in this book.

5. **Slow Down In Your Decision Making**

Somewhere in Western culture we have come to believe that "faster equals better". On the mystic's path, it is the exact opposite. Time needs to be given to all decisions being made to ensure the decision is optimal. I have found that having a desire but "not" acting on it immediately allows God time to assist me by bringing to me the resources or people I needed to manifest that desire. If we cannot wait for additional signs showing us that we are to move in a certain direction, it is likely our ego can take over the process and move us swiftly in a direction which may be hard to turn back from. Never be in too much of a hurry where you don't have room to give God time to work.

6. **Let Go of Planning Every Detail**

We are a society very preoccupied with planning every detail in our goal setting approach to life. As mentioned, the mystery and joy of life often happen in the spontaneity. From my spiritual readings as mentioned, this need to plan is a tool of the ego in order to control the outcome. Somewhere we have all bought into the idea that if we don't control every detail, the outcome will be undesirable or even terrible. This is simply not true. On the mystic's path, your job is simply to hold the vision, be obedient, and move as God directs, the details will be worked out.

7. **Trust Your Feelings**

On the mystic's path, you have heard other Modern Masters say that greatest asset is your feeling nature because it truly is your "intuitive guidance system". Whenever you make decisions outside of this system to either please others or to rush the manifestation, the outcome will always produce results that are less than desirable. It is only by feeling and expressing your true authentic emotionality that healing can take place and true guidance from the Spirit of God is possible. So always trust the feelings within you, they are never wrong.

8. **Use Your Dreams**

I have been blessed with the ability to hear my Spirit when it comes to interpreting my dreams. I shared one dream in the beginning of the book about the forest fire which was symbolic for my ego creating destruction. Therefore, know that dreams carry many hidden messages so it is important to pay attention to those dreams that seem to create intense emotionality within you. Upon waking, commune with your Spirit and trust what you are being told about the symbolism in your dream. If you do not have that kind of access just yet, find someone you trust to help you interpret the dream. The information gained will be invaluable.

9. **Own Your Contribution to the Chaos**

This is my favorite tip because it gave me the biggest results. Owning your contribution to the chaos simply means admit where you were wrong or failed to see another's point of view, made some assumptions or engaged in other behaviors that created conflict. Know that in all conflict, you are absolutely contributing something because of your view of reality. After you have fully expressed your anger, hatred or righteous position, take the time to find out what it was about that situation that really "pissed" you off. Now think about a time in your past where that has happened to you before and even journal about it. Continue this process until you can find the originating incident that causes you to react every time to similar stimulus. If it takes you back to childhood, then know you are getting to the root cause of your upset. Owning your contribution to the chaos will go a long way in bringing you peace of mind about the behavior of another.

10. Expand Your World View

Expand your worldview by traveling outside of your comfort zone. When we travel to places that we have never visited before, we tend to be more open. This is true for most of us because the newness tends to loosen the grip of the ego which thrives on routine and familiarity. Even if you don't have the funding to undertake the international travel that I mentioned in this book, allow yourself the pleasure of driving or flying to someplace that seems to pull at your heart strings. For in that place, you will find messages meant to move you along your mystic's path. Remember to take someone with you who understands your mystic's mindset. Expanding your reality through travel is an absolute must for the modern mystic.

Spiritual Guidance

We keep trying to live alone without the guidance from our Spirit. We are so focused on what we are trying to attain, we give God no room to operate within us. So even if we attain what we seek, we cannot sustain it. Our view of reality says we should pursue the things of this world, pursue the things in the "Land of Form", but we all know the things of this world cannot bring lasting peace and joy for they will surely pass away. You have read my story so you know from whence I speak. I speak from a place where I attained many of the values of this world, but the permanent fulfillment was not there. It was not there in having lots of money. It was not there in having the idealized relationship. It was not there in seeking more places in the world to visit. What we mystics are truly searching for is really inside of us.

In life coaching we are taught that when you look outside of yourself you see your own weaknesses reflected back to you in the behavior of others. However, when you look within you see the strength that comes from partnering with your Spirit. For those on a mystic's path, it is truly more important to be one with the Spirit of God within than to have the wealth of the world. What is ironic is that being one with the Spirit of God also gives you the wealth of the world. I lack for nothing in my life and any necessity for my human existence is provided for.

Life to me is like magic; I just think a thought and do nothing until I am told by my Spirit on how to proceed. The result is always optimal, even better than I imagined it would be. Many of us are programmed by our ego to set a goal and take a gazillion action steps to attain it. Living from that place will never allow for permanent sustainability because it will be built on fragmented reality. You can never know all of the variables that go into making the ultimate decision without having arrived at that choice point first. The other thing planning does besides limiting the way the Universe can respond to your requests is that it often comes at the expense of another's dreams. Only the Spirit of God within can tell you how to manifest your desires without negatively impacting someone else's desires.

For those on the mystic's path, the peace you desire is to align yourself with your Spirit then allow your Spirit to lead the dance. You will be amazed at the result. Your spiritual assignment is to "clean out the vessel" and calm the chatter in your mind to ensure you hear the voice of your Spirit with no distortions. It is time to for you to bring forward the "Chocolate Mystic" within and let the magnificence of God be made manifest in you.

Afterword

Part I is so deep, so honest, so real and accessible that I would be honored to translate it one day. I love the way your "stories" so naturally follow one another as if they were magically linked by this invisible thread. This book is bound to attract lots of readers because it is so real. I must say that I for one, although I already knew a lot of the special events in your life, just couldn't move away, until I had the book read. Thanks so much for sharing. The funny thing is that after reading Part I, I felt it had a healing in me, emotional wounds I never knew I had... Amazing stuff...

In Part II, you continued to show courage as you talked about your mystical experiences in exotic places like Italy, Thailand, Egypt, India, Israel and Peru. I know that you are not the only one out here having these mystical experiences because I too have experienced something unexplainable in Assisi that I want to share.

The approach was slow and easy, the breeze was cool and gentle, as I sat quietly in the car that was taking me to Assisi. The town floated in the distance and my mind held no particular expectation while my heart was perfectly at peace with itself. And then all of a sudden, without the slightest warning, I felt a shift in my world. Things were different and I was in a different place. And, in front of my very eyes, I saw coming from the town and towards me, what I can best describe as an enormous "gathering of souls". At the same time I felt myself leaving my body and floating towards them and eventually melting into them. From that union came an incredible feeling of unity, a total sense of belonging, extreme peace expressed in a way I never felt before. I knew then that I had come back "home" to loved ones; so I stayed, frozen in the moment, soaking in such wonderful light, beauty, peace and love…in short, the perfect delight of truly belonging.

The next day, the adventure continued while I took an early morning walk. Assisi was still asleep as I strolled down a deserted alley and heard a chorus of female voices. The call of their chants led me to an open chapel door covered by a curtain. I lifted the piece of cloth, walked in and was greeting by the questioning eyes of a handful of singing nuns. Oblivious to their furtive looks, I just followed their example and knelt down, promptly closing my eyes to better hear their angelic voices.

I could also sense a different type of energy in there, nothing I could really put my hands at first. And then, I knew that someone's remains kept us company, somewhere hidden under a rock. It also came to my knowledge that unwittingly; I had come here to pay my respects to this old soul which I knew in my heart to be St. Francis. So I did and soon after, I left as quietly as I had entered, with the feeling that I had accomplished a mission I had never consciously embarked on.

Later on that day, I was merely strolling along with a large crowd of tourists when I happened to look up and my eyes caught the eyes of a monk coming from the opposite direction. The minute I made eye contact with him, for a fleeting moment I felt I was swimming in the ocean of his eyes and saw a reflection of myself also dressed as a monk, in another lifetime, long, long ago.

The end of this very special weekend found me alone, on a mountain top, pondering over the mysteries of the unseen world. There, I sat on a rock, looking down at an exquisite valley of the Italian countryside, this time looking for yet another spiritual experience and requesting that God manifest his/her presence. I waited but nothing happened; and then, I heard a voice that told me, "Isn't all this quite enough for you?" Ashamed to have made such demands after being so blessed, I decided to let go of ego and just bask in the all beauty that Mother Nature had displayed all around me.

This lesson served me well because not only did I realize that spiritual experiences are not made to order, they just happen when you least expect them; and also I realized how fortunate I was to be conscious enough to see beyond the physical realm and appreciate yet another dimension of myself, the one that really matters. Let's all wake up to the limitless potential of any and every moment.

In closing, this book has left me in awe and has inspired me to write the following:

When words originate at The Source, they just keep coming
When Heaven dictates, the message is rendered indelible
When a messenger is inspired, all are invited to partake
When all eyes can see, not a thing remains hidden
When The Truth is out, it obliterates all darkness
When ego is gone, The Universal Light shines in once more

Danielle Bonnefil-Wahab
Teacher, Tri-Lingual Translator
Haiti/USA

About the Author

Robin L. Johnson is the founder of the Chocolate Mystic Society, an online spiritual community dedicated to helping ordinary people work through their emotional blockages to be able to own their mystical experiences. This combination of owning  both bitter and sweet experiences allows people to realign with the Spirit of God within and channel in a new way of being.

For 20 years, while acting as a management consultant, Ms. Johnson studied personal and spiritual development. She immersed herself in readings on the world's major religions including Christianity, Judaism, Islam, Taoism, Hinduism, and Buddhism. Ms. Johnson integrated her study of religion with travel to 40 countries where she had mystical experiences at sacred sites on five continents including Italy, Egypt, Israel, Thailand and Peru.

Ms. Johnson values education and has obtained the following degrees: BA, MA, MBA and Certificate in Life Coaching. Currently, Ms. Johnson who resides in suburban Philadelphia is a speaker, author and "mystic coach".

www.chocolatemysticsociety.com

Suggested Readings for Mystic's Journey

ACIMI, *A Course in Miracles*, Barnes & Noble Inc., China 2007

Braden, Gregg, *Fractal Time: The Secret of 2012 and a New World Age*, Hay House, Inc., New York 2009

Dyer, Wayne, Ph.D., *There's A Spiritual Solution to Every Problem,* HarperCollins, 2001

Dyer, Wayne, Ph.D., *Change Your Thoughts-Change Your Life: Living the Wisdom of the Tao*, Hay House, Carlsbad, CA, 2007

Ford, Debbie, *The Dark Side of the Light Chasers*, Riverhead Books (Division of Penguin Putnam), New York, 1998

Ford, Debbie, *The 21-Day Consciousness Cleanse: A Breakthrough Program for Connecting with Your Soul's Deepest Purpose,* HarperCollins, New York, 2009

Gawain, Shakti, *Living in the Light: A Guide to Personal and Planetary Transformation*, Nataraj Publishing (Division of New World Library), Novato, CA 1998

Goldsmith, Joel, *Practicing the Presence: The Inspirational Guide to Regaining meaning and a Sense of Purpose in Your Life*, Harper Collins, San Francisco, CA 1986

Hay, Louise, *You Can Heal Your Life*, Hay House, Carlsbad, CA, 1984

Hicks, Esther and Jerry, *Ask and It Is Given: Learning to Manifest Your Desires*, Hay House, Carlsbad, CA 2004

Maday, Michael (Editor), *New Thought for a New Millennium: Twelve Powers for the 21st Century*, Unity Books, Unity Village, MO 1998

Moses, Jeffrey, *Oneness: Great Principles Shared by All Religions*,
Ballantine Books, New York 2002

Myss, Carolyn, Ph.D., *Anatomy of the Spirit: The Seven Stages of Power and Healing*, Harmony Books, New York, NY 1996

Rasha, *Oneness*, Earthstar Press (Distributed by Hampton Roads Publishing Company) Charlottesville, VA 22902

Ruiz, Don Miguel, *The Four Agreements: A Toltec Wisdom Book*, Amber-Allen Publishing, San Rafael, CA 1997

Tolle, Eckhart, *A New Earth: Awakening to Your Life's Purpose*, Dutton (Penguin Group), New York 2005

Websites:

www.sourceofsynergyfoundation.org

www.lifephilosophy.co.za

www.create-you.dk

www.debbieford.com

www.chocolatemysticsociety.com

www.eomega.org

www.mishkaproductions.com

www.healyourlife.com